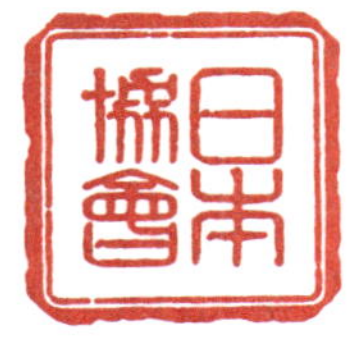

# JAPAN SOCIETY, INC.
## JAPAN HOUSE GALLERY

March 10, 1981


Ms. Kay Larson
New York Magazine
755 Second Avenue
New York, NY 10017


Dear Ms. Larson:

The Cleveland exhibition installation is almost finished here, and I am enclosing with this letter a hand-bound, advanced copy of the catalogue. Endpapers were not included in these copies, but I thought you might enjoy having one at this early stage anyway.

Opening to the public on March 19, I believe this exhibition beautifully demonstrates the strong leadership Sherman Lee provides us all. I hope you will have an early opportunity to come over.

With very best wishes,

Sincerely yours,

Rand Castile
Director

Enclosures


333 East 47th Street • New York, N. Y. 10017 • Telephone: (212) 832-1155

# ONE THOUSAND YEARS OF JAPANESE ART (650–1650)

## From The Cleveland Museum of Art

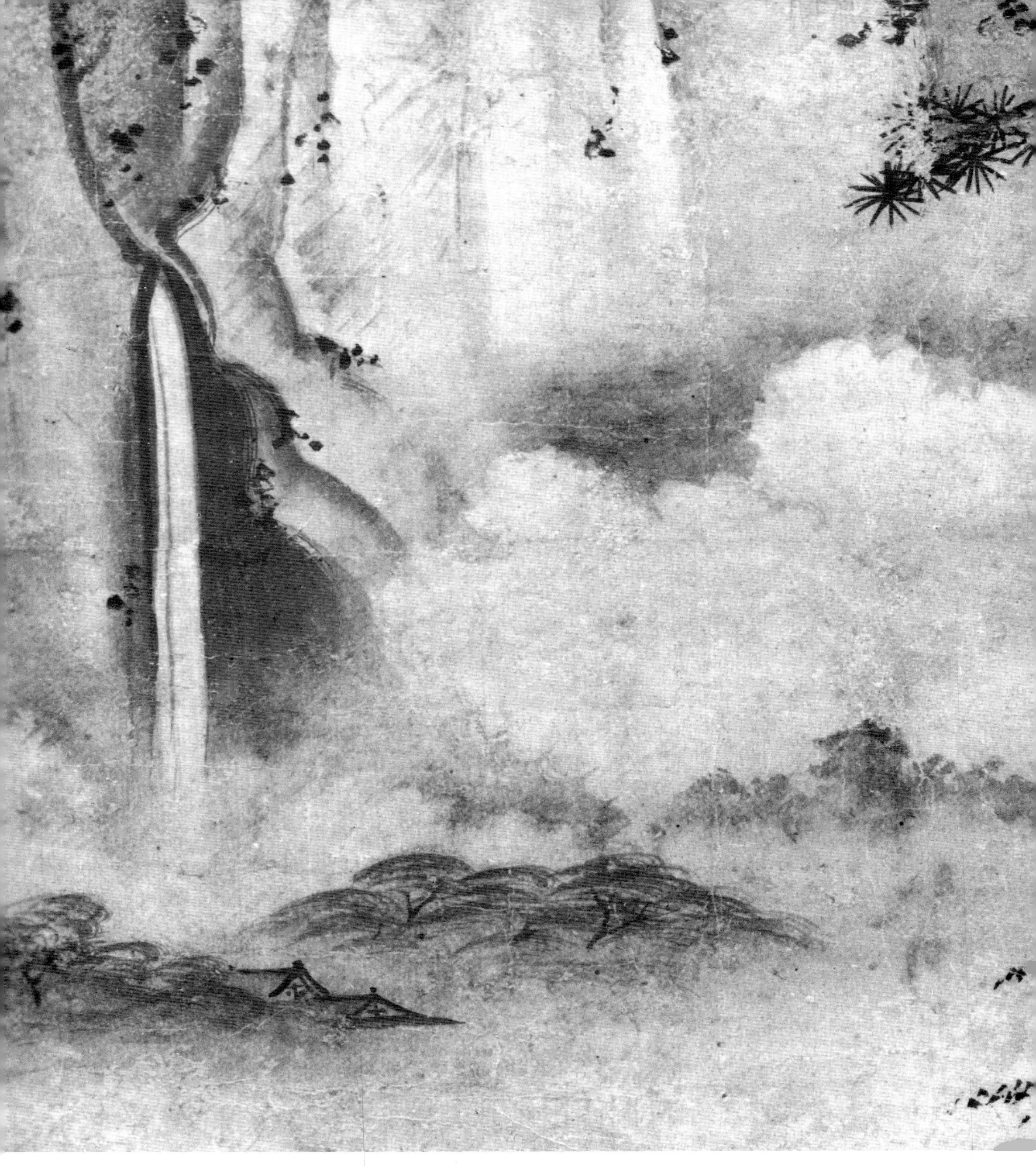

# ONE THOUSAND YEARS OF

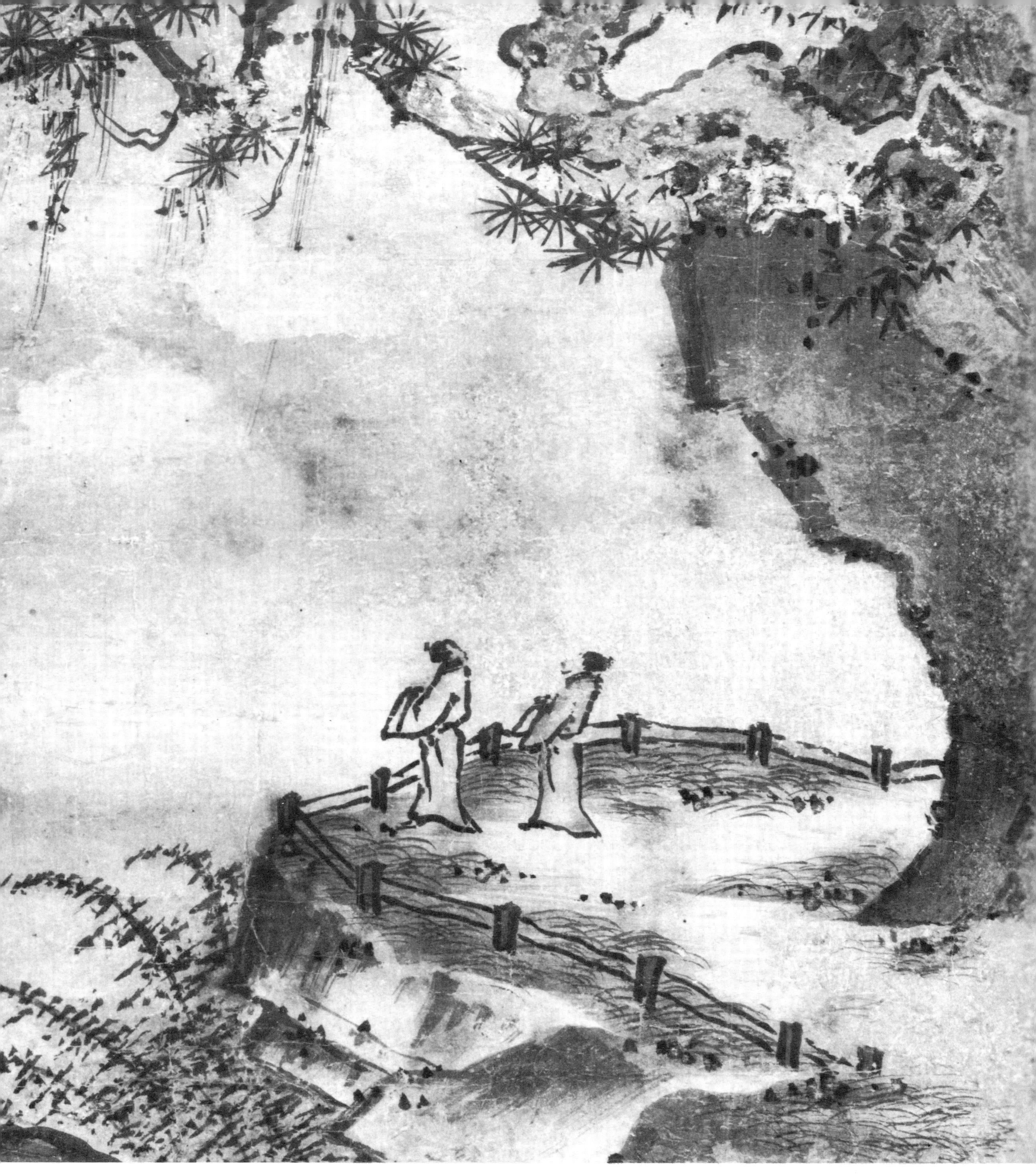

# JAPANESE ART (650–1650)

## From The Cleveland Museum of Art

Catalogue by Sherman E. Lee, Michael R. Cunningham, and Ursula Korneitchouck

Japan Society

ONE THOUSAND YEARS OF JAPANESE ART
is the catalogue of the exhibition of Japan House Gallery
shown in the spring of 1981 as an activity of the Japan Society.

Designed by Kiyoshi Kanai, New York, New York
Printed by Eastern Press, New Haven, Connecticut
Set in Palatino by LCR Graphics, New York, New York

Photographs courtesy of The Cleveland Museum of Art.
The dimensions of the paintings exclude mountings.

Library of Congress Catalogue Card Number 80-85323
ISBN 0-913304-12-3
Copyright © 1981 by the Japan Society, Inc.
Printed in the United States of America

All Japanese proper names are given in Japanese style, family
name first, given name last.

Cover illustration: Catalogue number 11, detail of Amida sculpture,
dated 1269, The Cleveland Museum of Art,
Purchase, John L. Severance Fund 60.197

# Contents

# Foreword

One thing that strikes the visitor to The Cleveland Museum of Art is the concern there with the representation and presentation, through a careful acquisition and exhibition policy, of *culture*. Culture. Not objects. Culture, as Webster would have it, as the complex of distinctive attainments, beliefs, and traditions which in long time yield a civilization. Of course there are the "masterpieces," the objects that tend to make museums famous, and among those at Cleveland one thinks immediately of Zurbarán's "House of Nazareth," Turner's "Burning of the Houses of Parliament," and, in this exhibition, the "Kumano Mandala" and Sesson's "Tiger and Dragon," and others.

The Cleveland Museum, while acquiring great works of art, has, it seems, paid careful attention to the representation of Japanese culture as manifested importantly by traditions. In Japan, as in most other ancient civilizations, it is ritual which connects one with the origins of civilization. The Cleveland Japanese collection and this exhibition include strong representations of four traditions: the temple rites of Japanese Buddhism; the simple but noble rituals of Shinto; the pervasive and profound tea ceremony; and the aristocratic dance of Nō theatre.

The Buddhist tradition is represented by the important "Miroku in Meditation" (cat. no. 1), a sculpture of mid-seventh century, a rare Asuka-Hakuhō bronze. A fine *Gigaku* mask, "Suikojū," (cat. no. 3) of the eighth century is specifically a Buddhist ritual object, a mask for the ancient dances at temples. Among the most important of Cleveland's Japanese Buddhist images is the painting of the late twelfth century depicting one of the "Secret Five" Bodhisattva (cat. no. 9). This Shingon sect piece is one of but five to survive, and the present version is the oldest. Among other sculptures in the exhibition, Buddhism is represented also by a dated "Amida" (cat. no. 11). This image is of the Tendai sect and contained at the time of its accession to the collection a complete sutra, list of donors, and a dedicatory inscription indicating not only the date of the work but the artists responsible for it.

Shinto ritual, too, is splendidly represented by objects of beauty and rarity. The two deities (cat. no. 6) formerly of the Usa Hachiman Shrine in Kyūshū were secret images. Made in the ninth or tenth century, these especially pleasing wooden sculptures are among the finest outside Japan. Another important Shinto sculpture is the Zaō Gongen (cat. no. 10) of the thirteenth century. The product of a mountain cult of ascetics, the Cleveland piece shares the characteristics of most Zaō Gongen sculptures but is exceptional in size. The Kumano Mandala (cat. no. 15) is a vivid Shinto recreation of a famous shrine and perhaps was used to prepare pilgrims for the sacred journey to the site or to remind them of the attributes of edifice, landscape, and visitors.

Continuing in this representation of the rituals of Japan, the tradition of tea ceremony has long been an interest of the Cleveland Museum and their collection of this art is strong. Dr. Lee directed an exhibition in 1963 at Asia House Gallery, "Tea Taste in Japanese Art", which drew upon Cleveland's extensive collection and other private and public American collections and did much to foster interest here in this unique art. Perhaps the principal means for the transmission of Japanese aesthetics over the last several hundred years, tea ceremony can be seen as *the* ritual of Japanese culture. While many of the hanging scrolls in the exhibition might be used for tea ceremony, we see most clearly the representation of the art form in the Cleveland ceramics. The outstanding tile in red Oribe ware (cat. no. 43) is justly famous. The Shigaraki jar (cat. no. 44) by the seventeenth century Kyoto artist Ninsei, the sixteenth century Shino and Bizen water jars (cat. nos. 41 and 40), and the outstanding "Dish with Three Wild Geese in Flight" (cat. no. 42) attest to The Cleveland Art Museum's distinction in this difficult area of connoisseurship.

The last of the four categories referred to above as ritual connecting us with the origins of a civilization is Nō. This ancient and profound form of drama is one of Japan's supreme contributions to world culture. Here, too, the Cleveland collections are rich. The mask is central in Nō to the drama and is sculpture of a high order.

Associated from early times with both Shinto and Buddhist rituals and performed for the common people, Nō came eventually to be performed at court and practiced as an art by the aristocrats. The masks from Cleveland here are of three distinct types: old man, young woman, and demon (cat. nos. 32, 33, 34). They are all from the Muromachi period (1392-1573). The mask in Nō is more than the servant-art of the theatre. It is central to the play, making ideal the character portrayed while manifesting by slight angling of the actor's head all the emotions required. The modeling of the mask and the uses of color surely derive from the sculptor's skill in Buddhist and Shinto sculpture making. These masks are among the finest outside Japan.

In the text of the *Shikadō-shō*, a treatise by the greatest theorist of Nō, Zeami, we find this observation: (Tsunoda Ryusaku, et. al., *Sources of Japanese Tradition,* New York, 1958, p. 299)

> The art of the accomplished veteran lies in the spiritual strength of his interpretations.

While a comment on the masters of Nō, this might apply as well to those who have guided the Cleveland Museum.

There are other, less ritualistic, traditions included in the exhibition. The work of important Kamakura and Muromachi ink painters—"The Poet Taira-no-Kanemori", one of the "Ten Fast Bulls", the elegant "Rock, Bamboo, and Orchids"—are examples. In addition, an outstanding fourteenth century handscroll, "Fukutomi Zoshi", the Tosa School screen of "Horses and Grooms in the Stable", the Sōami paintings, Shūbun, Sesson, and Kanō paintings extend still further the scope of the Cleveland collection.

Japanese art is one of the Cleveland Far Eastern collections, and what can be shown here is but a fraction of the whole. Still the representation shows well the strength of Cleveland. Japanese art has been a part of the museum since its opening in 1916, but it is important to note that by far the greatest part of this magnificent assembly was acquired by The Cleveland Museum of Art's current and preeminent Director and Curator of Oriental Art, Dr. Sherman E. Lee. Curator since 1952, Director since 1958, Dr. Lee, together with his colleagues Michael R. Cunningham and Ursula Korneitchouck, wrote the catalogue. Dr. Lee made the selection of works of art to be included. May we express the gratitude of the Japan Society and of the Japan House Gallery for his cooperation in every aspect of the exhibition. We are also grateful to Dr. Cunningham and Mrs. Korneitchouk for their assistance in bringing together an important selection of the collection for Cleveland's first Japanese exhibition in New York. Japan House Gallery is honored to enjoy this distinction.

The collections of The Cleveland Museum of Art are, ultimately, in the trust of that Board, and we extend our sincere appreciation to them and especially to the President, Mr. James H. Dempsey, Jr., for generously lending so many of the museum's treasures.

At the Gallery, the Advisory Committee on Arts is responsible for the development of exhibitions. Under the chairman, Mr. Porter A. McCray and with Dr. Lee as member, the committee continues to meet each year with an active agenda of proposed exhibitions. The Friends of the Gallery, with the leadership of Lily Auchincloss, concludes this year the tenth anniversary of its association. No more valuable services have been performed in support of this program than those of these two organizations.

Remarkably, in the changing museum world, most of the persons on the professional staff of Japan House Gallery have remained with us since the opening exhibition; Maryell Semal, Assistant Director and Registrar; Margot Paul, Assistant Director and Editor; Mitsuko Maekawa, Research and Coordinator. Hisayoshi Ota, Assistant to the Director, joined the staff last year. They, together with colleagues Cleo Nichols and Kiyoshi Kanai, form a team of which I am grateful to be a member.

Rand Castile
*Director*
*Japan House Gallery*

# The Japanese Collection at The Cleveland Museum of Art

The beginnings of the Japanese collection at The Cleveland Museum of Art date from at least one year before the public opening in 1916. Two Japanese sculptures, one of a standing Amida, the other of a sitting Yakushi, were acquired on June 10 and November 15, 1915, the former as a gift from D. Ushikibo of New York, the latter as a purchase with funds supplied by an early supporter of Far Eastern art, Worcester R. Warner. Both were soon determined to be late works of the Tokugawa period. On July 29, 1915, J. H. Donahey gave a sword guard to the museum. In 1916 a then modern hanging scroll of a lion by Suiseki Ohashi in the new realist style was given, and Mr. Warner contributed a nineteenth-century Nō robe with a wisteria design. The same donor gave a pair of Tokugawa period hanging scrolls with representations of birds and trees acquired from Mrs. Moncure Biddle. None of these early acquisitions occupy a meaningful place in the Japanese collections today.

However, on October 2, 1916, J. H. Wade bought for the museum from Yamanaka and Company, New York, a section of a seventeenth-century handscroll depicting a mob fleeing from a village fire, a work that is still of interest even if it but dimly mirrors similar scenes from the great handscrolls of the thirteenth century. And in 1917 Worcester Warner gave a fine Fujiwara blue and gold illuminated sutra scroll of the twelfth century, acquired from T. Kuroda, a work that maintains an honorable place in the first ranks of the permanent collection. Even more extraordinary was the acquisition from Professor John Strong Newberry of Columbia University of a very large bronze bell of the Yayoi period (300 B.C.-200 A.D.), still one of the few major works of pre-Buddhist art in the museum's Japanese collection. The *ukiyo-e* prints given in 1916 by Mr. and Mrs. J. H. Wade and Mrs. Henry S. Upson, eighty-two in all, included fine examples in good condition by Toyokuni and Utamaro among others.

This particular recital indicates what one might have assumed about the acquisitions by almost any American museum, outside Boston, pursuing Japanese art with less than complete enthusiasm. It might be noted here that of the forty-six Japanese works reproduced in the most recent publication of the Boston Oriental collection only ten percent were acquired since 1932; surprisingly the Freer handbook reveals that seventy percent of the major Japanese objects in that famous collection were purchased after that year. The new museum in Cleveland was primarily interested in Western art, and the development of Oriental collections depended upon individual donors and the knowledge and taste of the time. While friends of the museum, like Ralph King, knew Charles Freer and with him were able to acquire a few spectacular early Chinese stone sculptures, this friendship did not produce anything of comparable significance in the Japanese field, which was firmly controlled in America by Freer and by the succession of Oriental masters at the Museum of Fine Arts in Boston: Ernest Fenollosa, Okakura Kakuzo, and Denman Ross, among others. Outside these powerful pioneers, interest in Japanese art was confined to certain areas—prints, sword guards, netsuke and inrō, some late lacquers, late and heterogeneous types of ceramics, and what can only be called grotesqueries, backlashes from the wave of Japonisme that broke in Europe and New York in the late nineteenth century, such as uncomfortably realistic bears or wrestlers now unfortunately experiencing a revival in the present permissive art market.

A significant new name appears in the records of the Japanese collection at Cleveland in 1917—Langdon Warner. Retained on a largely informal basis as an advisor to the Cleveland Museum, Warner was to continue as an advisor, off and on, until 1938. Langdon Warner's keen interest in Japanese art and its techniques is well-known and it comes as no great surprise that he was instrumental in obtaining steel arrowheads and seventeen small wooden sculptor's models in 1917. The arrowheads testify to his belief that the simplest and most functional of art forms are significant, and the models to his recognition that the methods of the artists must be understood if one is to know their art. Two other of Langdon Warner's 1917 purchases are interesting. One is a hanging scroll "Kasuga Mandala" in color on silk showing Michizane riding the sacred deer with Buddhist deities embossed on the golden sun disc above. This splendid icon of the fourteenth century is a rare and beautiful work. The other acquisition was less fortunate but demonstrated both courage and perception—a fragment in the style of the "Frolicking Animals" scroll of Kōzan-ji with a seal purporting to be that of the temple. Both of these purchases reveal high purpose and a belief in the seriousness of Japanese art, a sharp contrast with the then dominant Western taste for miniature crafts and the always popular woodblock prints. This conviction was further demonstrated by the museum's publication of Langdon Warner's major study, *Japanese Sculpture of the Suiko Period,* in 1924.

The first gifts from D. Z. Norton also came in 1917. An indefatigable collector particularly interested in metalwork, Mr. Norton gave to the museum fifty-one bronze mirrors dating from the Fujiwara period and after. Later, he was responsible for the acquisition of a large and comprehensive collection of 297 sword guards.

Ralph King's penchant for major pieces, already mentioned in connection with the Chinese collection, is confirmed by a remarkable porcelain he gave in 1919, the large double-gourd shaped Imari vase with panels depicting a Dutch boat and sailors. This large, rare, and important work has become one of the most celebrated Namban porcelains known, reproduced in many modern publications on Namban art.

Thus, the first four years; and so the next fifteen. There were no additions outside the categories already established as characteristic for Japanese art. This is not a fault, for it was largely the same story elsewhere. The combination of Japanese protectiveness of their major works and the Western misconception that the Japanese genius was only for minatures and prints restricted the rational and significant development of Japanese collections such as that pursued by Boston, Berlin and, to a certain extent, Paris.

The Cleveland print collection was further enriched by J.H. Wade, and in 1930 Edward Loder Whittemore left his excellent collection, carefully built by purchases through Yamanaka and Company. This included marvelous Harunobu prints, two excellent actor portraits by Sharaku, and the unique pink mica background, "Physiognomic Study", one of the ten *Fujin Sogaku Jittai* Series by Utamaro. Another large group of works purchased at this time reveals a peculiarly characteristic Western taste for Japanese craftsmanship—258 stencils for textile patterns.

The first harbingers of other possibilities were a pair of *Kara-shishi* (Chinese lions), Shinto wood sculptures of fine quality and of the late Kamakura period, acquired by purchase in 1924. Ten years later the first really major work of Japanese secular painting was acquired on the recommendation of the Curator of Oriental Art, Howard Coonley Hollis, a Harvard pupil of Langdon Warner, who had been appointed to his post in 1930 by the second Director, William Mathewson Milliken. The purchase of the horse screens (cat. no. 25) was a major event, for they are one of the best and earliest of their type. But this excellent beginning was aborted by the growing tensions of Japanese political and military affairs as well as by the increasingly protective attitude of the Japanese authorities entrusted with cultural property. Few Western museums made major Japanese acquisitions in the late nineteen-thirties. The last major work that Cleveland acquired during this period was from Langdon Warner in 1938—a large, complex, and excellent hanging scroll representing *Yakushi and the Twelve Generals* of the Kamakura period. Then the war began, raising a true "great divide" in the understanding and collecting of Japanese art.

During the war almost all museums retired or closed their Japanese collections—usually citing the possibility of misguided aggression and consequent unacceptable danger levels for irreplaceable works of art. This was true, but it was not the whole story. The thirties had seen little growth in American collections of Japanese art in part because of the Japanese protectiveness already mentioned, but also because of an undeniable American prejudice against the Japanese themselves. Further, Americans found it comfortable to think of the Japanese as patient copyists of, first, China, and then the West. Far Eastern studies in general, but Japanese studies in particular, were not high on the priority lists of American education. I remember well the visit to the Cleveland Museum's storage of a very famous Harvard scholar of European art who, observing Howard Hollis and me working on a Chinese ceramic exhibition, called out, only half in jest: "Still bothering with the Orient?"

The war changed all this, particularly in the Pacific theatre. Dislike of the enemy was gradually tempered by grudging respect. Hundreds of future specialists took crash courses in Chinese and Japanese. But the postwar Occupation was far more important. Despite the usual sad incidents of conquering arrogance, impenetrable misunderstanding, and sheer thoughtlessness, the rotation of both civilian and military personnel exposed hundreds of thousands of Americans to an ancient and proud civilization, particularly to that great majority of the Japanese population who earnestly and intelligently worked for a reconstructed society which would preserve those elements of the past so much a part of any great creative and peaceful nation. The avidity of Japanese participation in the free and open art exhibitions, concerts, theatre, and the new wave of literature could not but impress the Westerners. In short the Occupation was as much an education for the Allies, particularly the Americans, as it was for the Japanese.

The results of these new cultural forces and interests were quick to appear in American art museums, including the one in Cleveland.

The Japanese need for bare subsistence and then for economic growth made the export regulations for cultural property more flexible, always excepting the some 8,000 objects offically registered for special protection. For the first time excellent and sometimes major works of Japanese art were collected for our museums. It should be recognized, however, that the great early Buddhist paintings and sculptures of the Heian period, so characteristic of the early part of the Boston collection, were no longer available for export. Howard Hollis was for one year the officer in charge of the Arts and Monuments division of the Occupation headquarters. After that, he resigned as Curator at The Cleveland Museum of Art to become a dealer in Far Eastern art. From him the museum acquired a number of classic Japanese works of art, beginning in 1949 with the single-panel screen by Sōtatsu, the "Crossing at Sano Ford," based on a poem by Fujiwara Teika. In the same year came the Tempyō *Gigaku* mask (cat. no. 3) and in the following year these other major early works: the Bronze Miroku from the Hashimoto collection (cat. no. 1) the clay figure of a woman from the pagoda base at Hōryū-ji (cat. no. 2); and the lovely *gyōdō* mask of a bodhisattva (cat. no. 8). In 1951 the museum selected a section of the Agedatami set of thirty-six poets (cat. no. 12) and a leaf from the Ise Monogatari album by Sōtatsu formerly in the Inoue collection and exhibited here at Japan House Gallery in its first Rimpa exhibition.

The museum in 1952 made a firm committment to a still more active development of the Japanese collection by appointing a Curator of Oriental Art, a position vacant since 1949. I say more active since one of the conditions under which the position was filled was the understanding by both Curator and Director that the Oriental collections needed a strong, reasoned and continuing development so that they might be more comparable with the already outstanding collections of ancient, medieval, and modern Western art. This we have tried to do, insofar as the fluctuations of the art market permitted. These fluctuations were in prices and availability. The late forties and fifties provided extraordinary opportunities for buying at reasonable prices certain kinds of Japanese objects—notably Kamakura Buddhist painting (cat. nos. 9, 14, 15, 19), large screens (cat. nos. 26, 36), and porcelains (none of these are shown here, including the splendid collection given the museum in 1965 with life interest reserved by Mr. and Mrs. Severance A. Millikin). The sixties and seventies were marked particularly by a steady rise in prices which had an unexpected benefit, for it restored the health and breadth of the Japanese art market. Where before there had been a few old-time dealers and collectors there were now many new and important ones. Some of these were specialized in their interests. Dealers in tea ceremony utensils seldom collect Buddhist sculptures or oversize pictures and screens. Specialists in later Japanese painting are now appearing. We cheerfully signal here the importance of these dealers for museums and collectors. Many of them are knowledgeable scholars or sensitive connoisseurs, or both, and their educational services are usually underrated, particularly in terms of the physical handling of original material.

Now many more ink paintings appeared (cat. nos.

22, 23, 26, 28, 35), as well as early stonewares (cat. no. 31) and the highly prized tea ceremony wares and utensils (cat. nos. 30, 40-44). Perhaps our decision to pay the necessary prices for the tea wares, still difficult for many Westerners to appreciate, was a reaffirmation of our determination to show as much as possible of what the Japanese—and now Western Orientalists—considered to be among the most creative Japanese achievements. The Ashiya iron kettle (cat. no. 30) is the most recent and perhaps the most arcane of these acquisitions. While one can never hope to rival the wonders of a Hatakeyama, Nezu, Matsunaga or Yamato Bunka museums, much less those in the three great national museums in Tokyo, Kyoto, and Nara, one can try to provide a taste of this rarified brew. Without it no collection can be truly Japanese.

This is no new idea. Others, both now and in the past, have achieved it. We can speculate on what might have happened if the splendid, intelligent, and tasteful work of Kummel at Berlin, Fenollosa, Okakura and Ross at Boston, Bosch-Reitz at New York, or Charles Freer, had been steadily built upon by their successors in the twenties. The Great Depression and World War II put such possibilities to rest. In the forty-five years since the war numerous museums, especially those at Seattle, New York, Kansas City, Chicago, Honolulu, and Washington, have succeeded with major collecting in various fields of Japanese art. Private collectors such as Mr. and Mrs. Jackson Burke, Harry Packard, Kimiko and John Powers, Mr. and Mrs. Joe Price, and Mr. and Mrs. John D. Rockefeller 3rd, have made superb assemblages of varying aspects of Japanese art. Exhibitions of their collections have been held in recent years, and the response of public and scholar alike has been enthusiastic.

The increasing number of Japanese art exhibitions, especially those with more specialized and coherent themes, both attest to this interest and stimulate it through a truly educational process—one that involves learning and enjoying by looking at and comparing original works of art. The Cleveland Museum was able to present numerous exhibitions of this kind: *Japanese Decorative Style* in 1963, *Japonisme* in 1975, *Japanese Screens* in 1977, *Folk Traditions in Japanese Art* in 1978, as well as exhibitions of contemporary ceramics, prints, and the art of packaging. This museum is proud of its part in this continuing process. The current exhibition of a selection from one chronological segment of the history of Japanese art should be understood not merely as a proud display but as a thankful offering to the artists and culture of Japan.

Sherman E. Lee
*Director and Chief Curator of Oriental Art*
*The Cleveland Museum of Art*

# Plates and Catalogues

1

## Miroku in Meditation

*Asuka Period, 7th century*
*Bronze*
*H. 39.4 cm.*
*Ex collection: Hashimoto Kansetsu, Kyoto*
*Purchase, John L. Severance Fund 50.86*

Miroku, the Buddha of the Future, but shown as a bodhisattva (hence not yet a Buddha) in pensive pose with the right leg crossed over the hanging left one, and with the tips of the fingers of the right hand just touching the chin, was one of the most popular of images in the early days of Buddhism in Japan. The unusual pose, so different from the more hieratic and balanced conformations of most Buddhist images, has endeared itself to modern Japanese and Westerners alike. The most famous and often reproduced images of early Buddhist art in Japan are the wooden Miroku representations of the seventh century at the nunnery, Chūgū-ji, next to Hōryū-ji in Nara, and at Kōryū-ji in western Kyoto. In this success they have fulfilled their iconic purpose, for they are, above all, images of compassion and receptivity, infinitely merciful and accessible to all who approach. Miroku in the *Hanka-shiyui* pose was most popular in the seventh century; but after that, few if any images of the type are known. This can be explained in part by the growing acceptance and formulation of Buddhism in Japan, but geographic considerations also play a part.

The pose originated in sixth century China in representations of Shakyamuni, the historic Buddha, particularly at that moment just after he made the decision to leave the luxurious life of his father's court. The pose was then used for Shakyamuni and his heavenly counterpart Prabhuturatna in representations of their meeting and joint conversation-meditation. The transfer of the pose to Maitreya (in Chinese *Mi-to-lo;* in Japanese *Miroku*), the Buddha of the Future, may well have occurred in China but the earliest extant images clearly identifiable as Maitreya are from Korea dating to the Silla period (668-935). These are the images that directly inspired the Japanese ones—whether produced from Korean prototypes or by Korean artisans on Japanese soil.

These early bronze images are highly prized in Japan today and most of them are registered objects, many at Hōryū-ji or in the Imperial Collection given to it by that temple. Hōryū-ji was the fountainhead of Buddhism in Japan due to the patronage of the royal prince Shōtoku Taishi who was the historically successful instrument for Buddhism's triumph in Japan after its introduction in 552. The present sculpture is a representation of the Asuka-Hakuhō bronze image type, rare outside Japan. While there are more than a few Miroku images at Hōryū-ji and in the Imperial Collection, the closest parallel to this one in pose, costume and style is that in the Masaki Museum in Osaka. Both sculptures are missing original pedestal bases.—SEL

Published:

Museum of Fine Arts Boston, *Illustrated Catalogue of a Special Loan Exhibition of Art Treasures from Japan* (Boston, 1936), cat. no. 6.

Shimizu Zenzō, "Japanese Sculptures in America and Canada," *Ars Buddhica,* 126 (September 1979): 70, fig. 10.

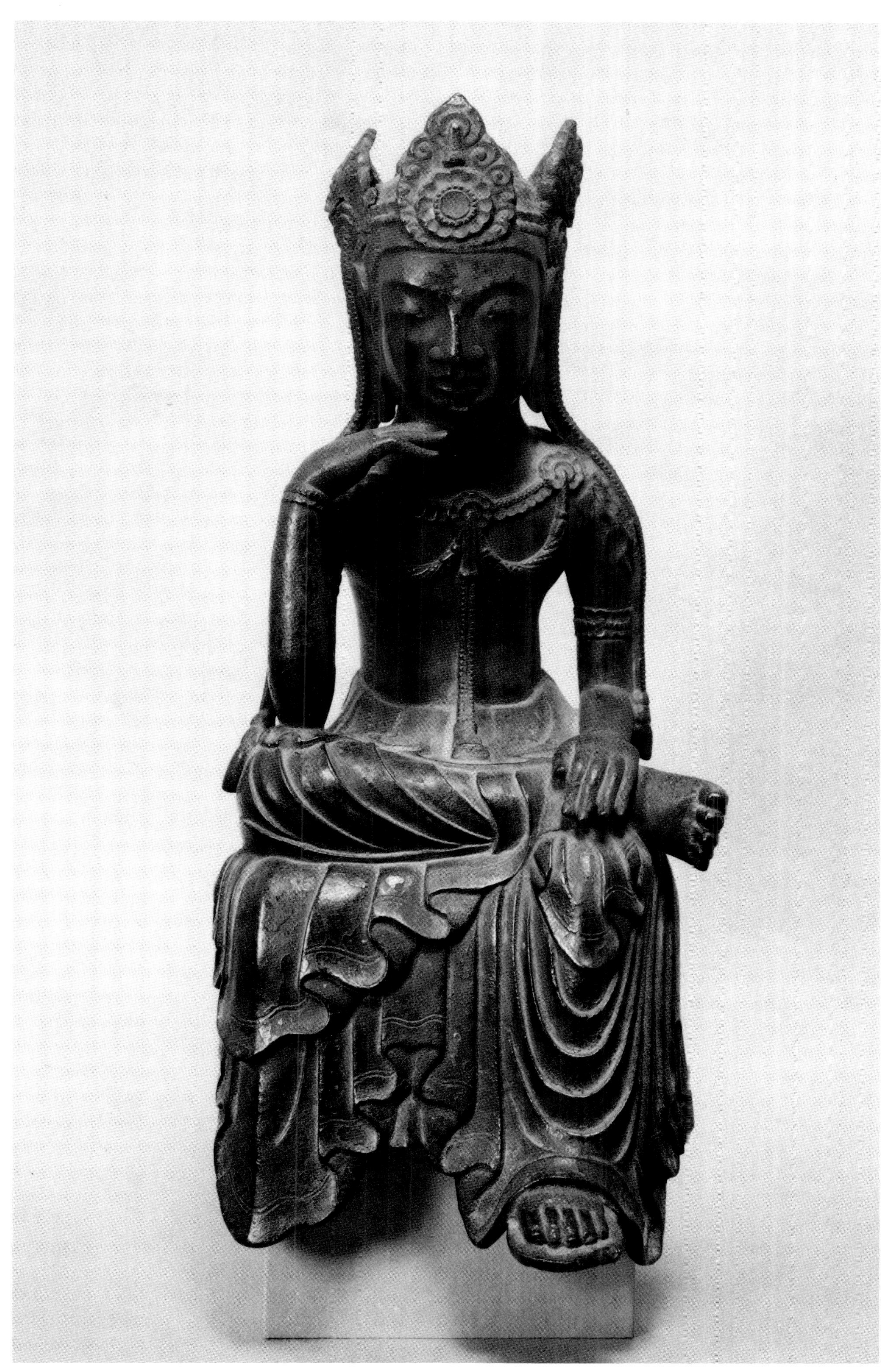

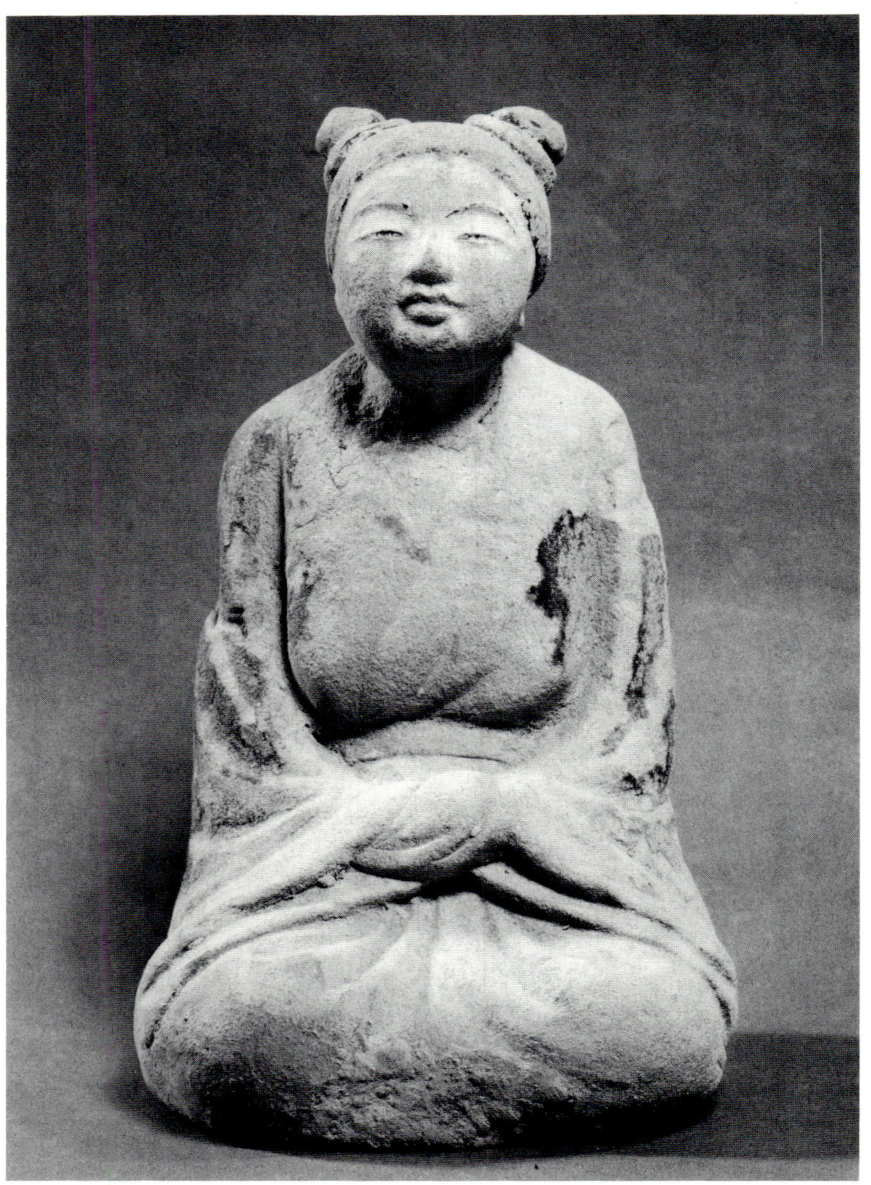

2

## Woman from an Audience Scene

*Hakuhō Period, 645-710*
*Gray unfired clay*
*H. 19 cm.*
*Provenance: probably from Hōryū-ji, Nara*
*Ex collection: Moriya K., Kyoto*
*Purchase, Edward L. Whittemore Fund 50.393*

The five storied pagoda (Gojū-no-tō) of Hōryū-ji is now generally considered to have been rebuilt after the disastrous fire of 670, but before 693 when the temple complex was in full use. The pagoda was a Far Eastern version of the Indian *stupa,* a mound commemorating the passing away (Nirvana) of the Buddha. At Hōryū-ji the ground floor interior of the pagoda contains four sculptured groups in clay dating from 711 A.D., representing the following: East, *The Debate between Manjusri and Vimalakirti;* West, *The Distribution of Shakyamuni's Ashes;* North, *The Nehan* (Nirvana of the Buddha); and South, *The Land of Miroku.* While some ninety figures with their mountain landscape backgrounds remain, most have been re-worked. Some were removed about 1900 and have found their way into Japanese private collections. This one, perhaps from the Northern or Southern groups, came to Cleveland from the Moriya collection in Kyoto in 1950.

Traces of color are still present and originally the figure, like its partners, must have looked very much like Sui or early T'ang dynasty tomb figurines with slip and color decoration. The clay is either dried or fired at a very low temperature. It is sandy and fragile, supported on the interior by a wooden stick with wire wrappings, visible only by X-ray analysis, and by a wooden slab base imbedded in the clay. The face has been slightly reworked and the head itself was broken at the neck and is re-attached. Still, the easy pose of the figure and its worldly expression are characteristic of the international style of Buddhist art in the Far East under the domination of Chinese Imperial art of the Sui and early T'ang dynasties. This small figure is a rare and precious relic from the most important early Buddhist site in Japan.—SEL

Published:
Shimizu Zenzō, "Japanese Sculptures in America and Canada," *Ars Buddhica,* 126 (September 1979): 71, fig. 17.

3

## Suikojū: Gigaku Mask

*Late Nara Period, 710-794*
*Wood (paulownia) with lacquer and paint*
*H. 28 cm.*
*Purchase, John L. Severance Fund 49.158*

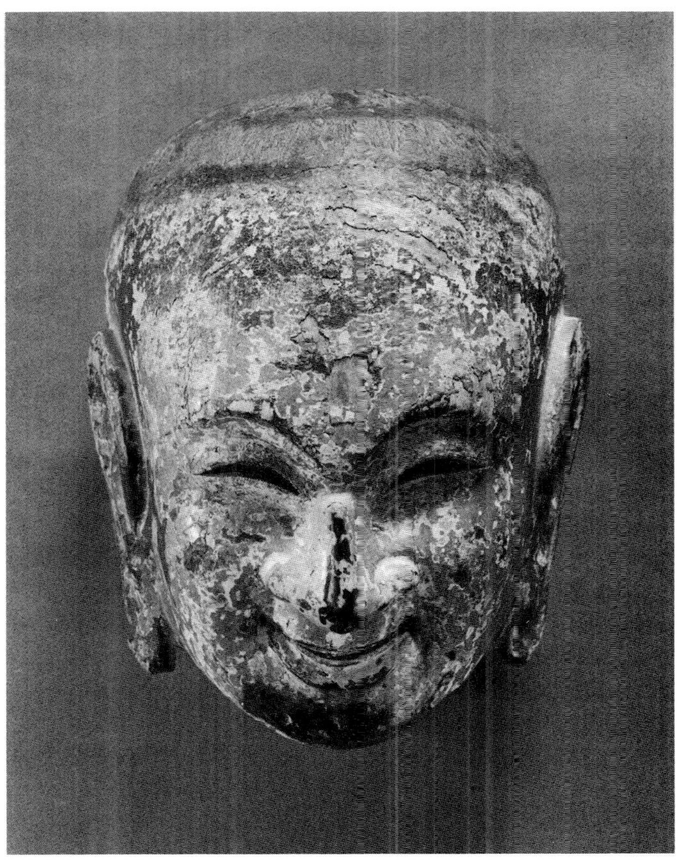

Imperial patronage of Buddhism in Japan reached its zenith in the eighth century under the leadership of Emperor Shōmu (724-749). With the transfer of the capital to Nara, a series of monumental building projects commenced, both secular and religious. Some of the buildings survive today and are great attractions to vistors of Nara.

During this Tempyō period Buddhist art in Nara, and indeed throughout the islands of Japan, flourished as never before—or since. Each of the large Buddhist monastic institutions in Nara had among its various administrative offices a department for the production and maintenance of sculpture. Here master sculptors and their assistants labored to fill orders for images of metal, clay, dry lacquer, and wood. The largest *zōbutsu-sho* (office for sculpture-making) was located at the Tōdai-ji, Nara's largest, imperially-sponsored temple. It was here that the dedication ceremony for the colossal bronze Buddha was performed in May 752. Included among the many activities associated with this event were performances of *Gigaku*.

A religious drama incorporating the use of music and dance, *Gigaku* is said to have been introduced into Japan from China and Korea by the seventh century. Performed to the accompaniment of flute, gong, and drum, *Gigaku* began during the eighth century as part of Buddhist religious services and evolved to court-sponsored, semi-comic dance performance. The music was played by musicians from the official bureau of music, and the dancers wore masks provided by the *zōbutsu-sho* sculptors.

Normally twenty-one masks formed a set for *Gigaku*. Traditionally this mask is said to represent Suikojū, one of the eight drunken attendants accompanying Empress Suiko (also inebriated), appearing at the end of the performance in a dance called *harameki*. The mask is carved from a single piece of paulownia wood into which holes have been drilled for shaping eyes, mouth, and nostrils. In addition, a series of small holes remain exposed along the mask's back edges indicating that originally tassels of hair or cloth were attached to the back and side of the mask, thereby concealing the entire head of the dancer. Further realistic touches included the application with lacquer of three layers of hair to the top of the mask, hair and eyebrows drawn in black ink, silvered teeth, reddened mouth, and the careful preparation of the entire mask surface with succeeding layers of lacquer, gesso, and tinted pigments of yellow, red, and blue-green. Time and wear have damaged the hair and some of the surface coloring here.

Each of the eight drunken *Suikojū* seen during a performance possessed individual comic movements and features, enhanced by the mask's "foreign" appearance. In fact among the masks surviving in Japan at the Hōryū-ji, Shōsōin, Imperial Household, and National Museum collections, a number of Suikojū types can be detected from within a broader classification identifying *Gigaku* masks according to medium (wood or dry lacquer), surface preparation, provenance, or the presence of inscriptions. Comparison with these other *Suikojū* masks suggests that this Cleveland piece belongs to an elaborately carved group, frequently bearing inscriptions by the carver or a later restorer, and originally associated with the Tōdai-ji or Hōryū-ji temples in Nara. Recent inspection of the mask revealed a two-line inscription, decipherable only in part as yet, overlooked for the thirty-year period since the mask's acquisition. In addition, a reasonable case can be made for questioning the traditional identification of this mask as representing *Suikojū*. Comparison of facial characteristics and carving style with *Shishiko* and *Taikoji Gigaku* masks reveal many similarities.

While further study continues on the inscription and precise identity of the mask itself, it is to be admired as one of a handful of eighth-century masks in public collections in the West. It represents not only a glorious period of sculptural achievement in Japanese art, but also a compelling example of the oldest surviving mask-carving tradition in the world.—MRC


Published:

Peter Kleinschmidt, *Die Masken der Gigaku der Altesten Theaterform Japans* (Weisbaden, 1966), no. 103.

Shimizu Zenzō, "Japanese Sculptures in America and Canada," *Ars Buddhica* 126 (September 1979): 74, fig. 29.

Kurata Bunsaku, ed., *Chōkoku*, Zaigai Nihon no Shihō, vol. 8 (Tokyo, 1980), no. 93.

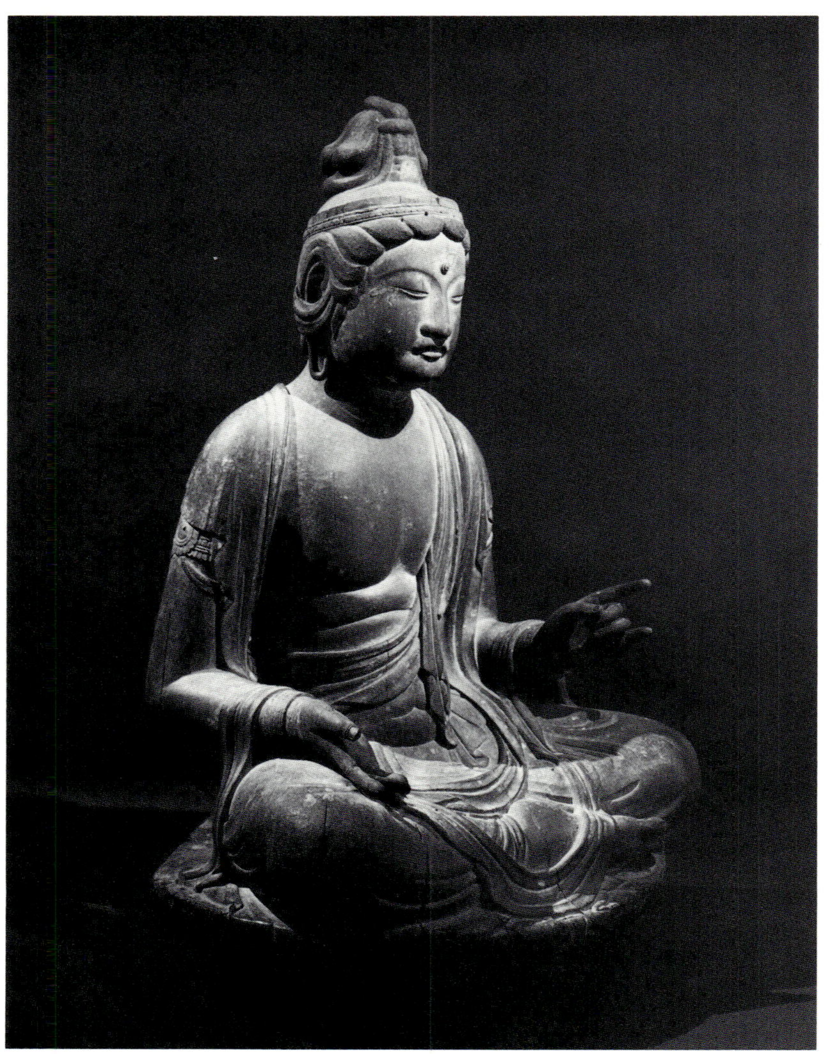

4

Nikkō, the Sun Bodhisattva

*Early Heian Period, ca. 800*
*Wood; carved from one block of yew*
*H. 46.7 cm.*
*Purchase, John L. Severance Fund 61.48*

Carved around 800, this wood sculpture shows the fully-absorbed international Chinese T'ang style of late Nara Japan at its finest, while anticipating the idealism of the early Heian period. It also displays the peculiarly Japanese affinity for natural material, surpassing the few surviving Chinese wood sculptures in this style brought to Japan before the destruction of Buddhist art in China during the period of persecution after 845.

The figure sits cross-legged on a lotus flower. A golden disk adorning its top-knot identifies it as Nikkō, the Sun Bodhisattva, suggesting that it once was part of a traditional triad comprising Yakushi, the healing Buddha, with Nikkō to the left and Gakkō, the Moon Bodhisattva, to the right. Nikkō's face, with eyes sympathetically cast down on the supplicant and with an enigmatic sad-sweet smile on his lips, radiates compassion—the very essence of early Buddhism. This compassion is serenely detached—aloof and aristocratic. The figure, though well-fleshed, is graceful and carefully detailed; even the cuticles are carved on the delicate fingers. The flowing rhythm of the draperies captures the lightness of the fabric in the skirt, shawl and scarves. One end of the scarf draped across the chest is brought forward over the shoulder, then nonchalantly looped up in front—a lively detail which, in addition to its visual charm, helps in dating the sculpture, for it occurs in few other works, all from the last years of the eighth century or the first decades of the ninth. Other telling details are the two strands of hair looping back over the lower ear and the short, pointed lock hanging in front, the loosely hanging lower chains of the armlets, the striated lotus petals and the wave-like treatment of the drapery ridges. Except for the hair, probably once blue but now darkened, and for the gilding on the jewelry, the statue was never painted. It is a "single-block" sculpture (as opposed to the later "joined-block" technique), carved from tight-grained yew in the T'ang tradition of the Chinese. A drill-hole and mortise joint on the base and nail holes around the diadem remind us of two separately carved attachments, now missing: a high crown and a body halo (mandorla).—SEL/UK


Published:

Sherman E. Lee, "Nikkō, the Sun Bodhisattva," *The Bulletin of The Cleveland Museum of Art* 48, no. 10 (1961): 259-265, figs. 1-3.

John M. Rosenfield, *Japanese Arts of the Heian Period* (New York, 1967), cat. no. 11.

Shimizu Zenzō, "Japanese Sculptures in America and Canada," *Ars Buddhica,* 126 (September 1979): 69, fig. 6.

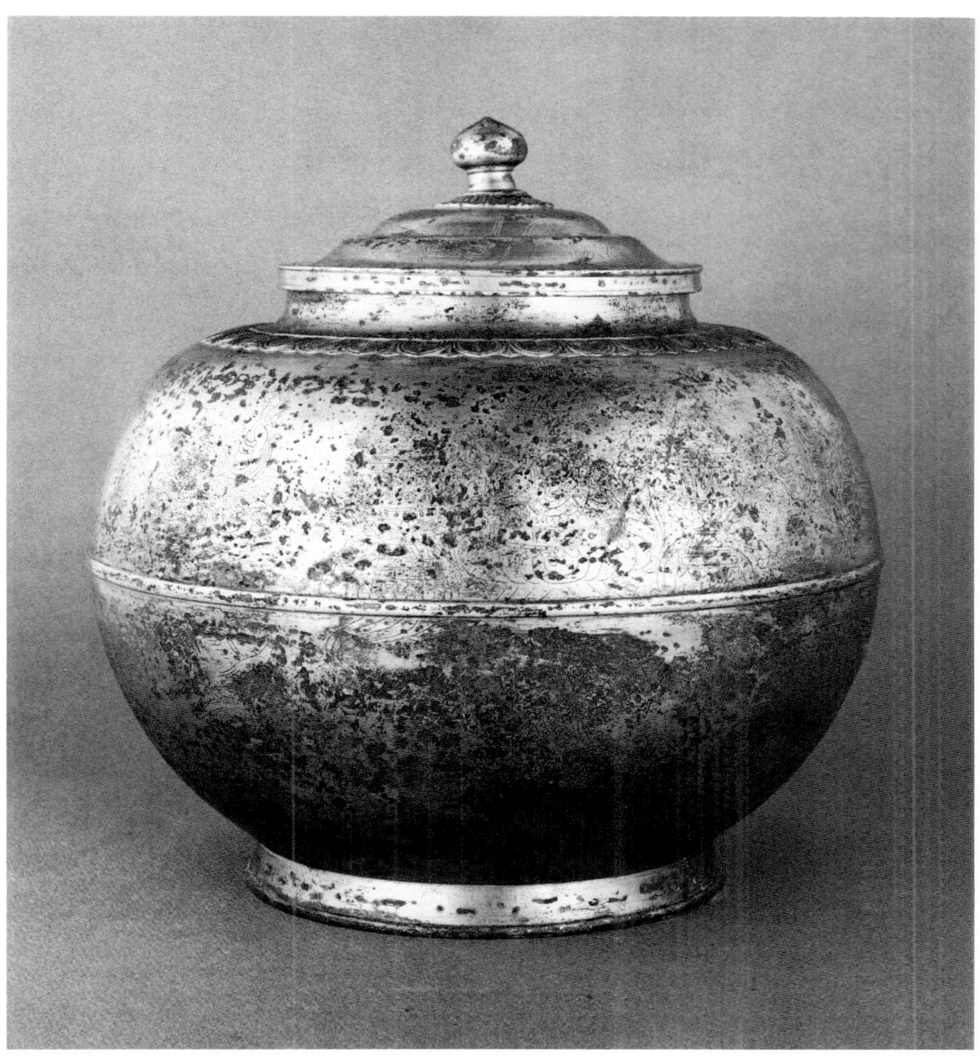

5

## Cinerary Jar with Scenes from the Western Paradise

*Heian Period, 9th-10th centuries*
*Gilt bronze with incised designs*
*H. 26 cm.*
*Ex collection: Inoue K.*
*Purchase from the J. H. Wade Fund 60.55*

This gilt bronze covered jar is most likely a cinerary urn used for the ashes of a particularly wealthy and well-connected person. There is yet another, but more remote, chance that it contained Buddhist relics put with a foundation deposit beneath a new building such as a pagoda. In any case it has been buried and the cover is clearly a later replacement though in harmony with the lower part and probably close in shape to the original. The shape is related to others of the T'ang dynasty in China and the Tempyō period in Japan. The proportions have been modified however in favor of a horizontal orientation and this, combined with the more linear and low relief character of the lotus petal ornament on the shoulder—indicate a date as early as the ninth century but conceivably as late as the eleventh.

This later dating is somewhat confirmed by the nature of the incised decoration on the body of the vessel. The upper register shows four celestial scenes: a Buddha with attendant bodhisattvas on clouds; an octagonal hall with four subsidiary buildings; and two scenes of small palace-type buildings. At least two of the attendant bodhisattvas are shown in almost three-quarters view from behind, a sophisticated and realistic device one would normally associate with the period of the development of *raigō* scenes (visions of the Amida Buddha coming from the Western Paradise) in the eleventh century. There are parallels here to the cover illustration of a Western Paradise scene in scroll twelve of the well known eleventh century set of sutra scrolls donated by the Heike family and kept at Itsukushima Shrine.

The lower register shows wild beasts and humans, probably indicating the realm of earth and the recurring wheel of life. In the division between Heaven and Earth one sees an early manifestation of the more elaborate symbolism to be seen in the "Nika Byakudō" painting (cat. no. 14) of the early Kamakura period. This vessel, with its elaborate and carefully executed design, is a particularly rare example of the sumptuous and elegant techniques and materials characteristic of the Heian period.—SEL

Published:

Sherman E. Lee, *Japanese Decorative Style* (Cleveland, 1961), cat. no. 12.

John Rosenfield, *Japanese Arts of the Heian Period* (New York, 1967), cat. no. 26.

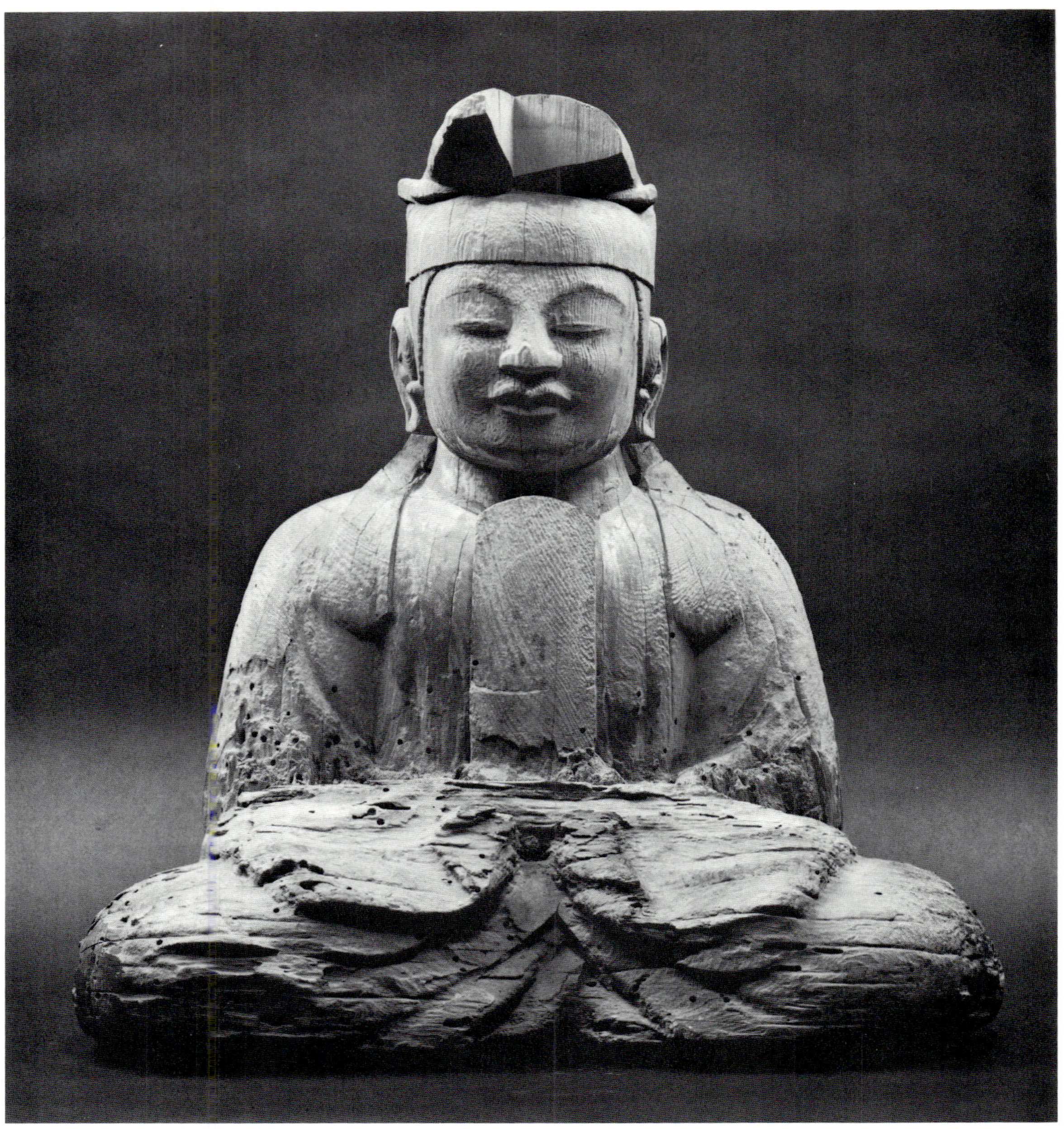

6

## Shinto Deities

*Early Heian Period, 9th-10th century*
*Wood (yew)*
*Male H. 53.3 cm. Female H. 50.3 cm.*
*Provenance: Shrine of Usa Hachiman, Ōita prefecture*
*Purchase, Leonard C. Hanna Jr. Bequest 78.3-.4*

Before the introduction of Buddhism into Japan in the sixth century an indigenous religion called Shinto had thrived for several centuries. Comprised of religious beliefs, folk traditions, and social-political attitudes which were then evolving in the young nation, objects of worship in Shinto did not exist at first. But with the realization that credibility of political stature could be enhanced through identification with popular religious customs, symbols were created to help convey Shinto visually. The first three of these are believed to be the sacred mirror, sword, and jewel, all of which survive to this day as talismans of the Emperor and his family.

In Japan these imperial treasures are enshrined in magnificent Shinto edifices, in contrast to the many thousands of modest shrines for local deities found throughout the country. Shrines are erected for the deity *(kami)*, of a particular village, neighborhood, or place—be it vast or small. To the early Japanese sites in nature could be as sacred as "things," and shrines of varying sophistication were erected to acknowledge the presence of *kami*.

The arrival of Buddhism and its acceptance by increasing numbers of people posed serious competitive problems for Shinto's continued viability, especially since Buddhism already possessed sophisticated visual imagery useful for illustrating and promoting its religious concepts. As a consequence Shinto resorted to portraying its *kami*. These two Cleveland images were formerly part of a set of five such secret images *(hibutsu)* of the Usa Hachiman Shrine in Ōita prefecture, Kyūshū.

The seated figures represent a male and female *kami* portrayed as members of court rather than as Buddhist deities, as was often the case. The male figure *(hikogami)* is clothed in

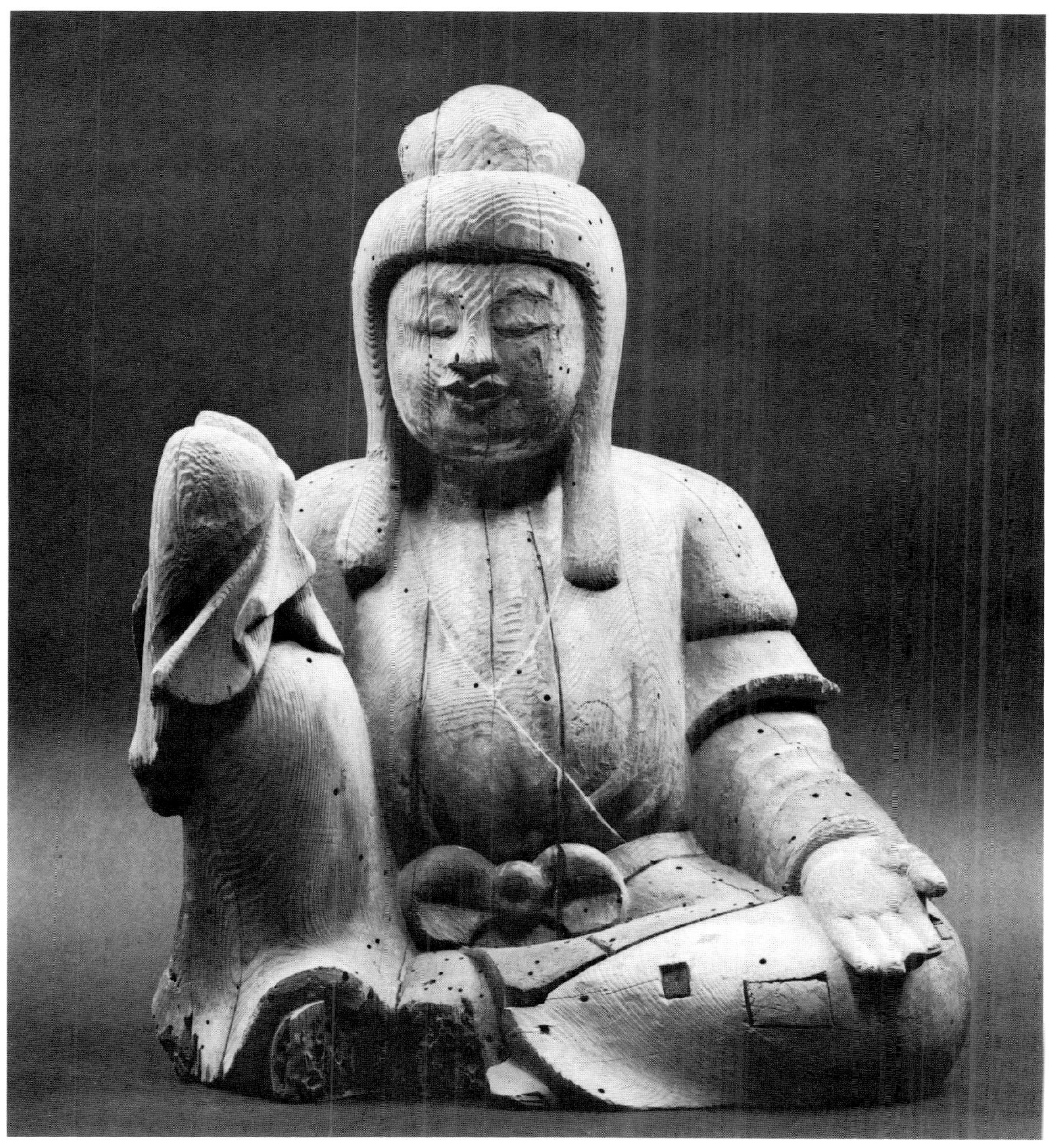

courtly apparel, much of which has been lost in the frontal area over the lap due to water and insect damage. The wooden cap with two appendages at the rear trailing over both shoulders describes the formal court hat of stiff black-lacquered cloth. The wide scepter *(shaku)*, an emblem of high social rank and authority, was once painted white. Indeed both figures have lost nearly all traces of the bright colors that once covered them. Only small areas of a white preparatory ground remain.

The female figure *(himegami)* wears T'ang-style robes and coiffure similar to images of the Buddhist deities Bonten and Benzaiten. One hand is hidden clutching some robe folds, an iconographic feature present in some Buddhist sculpture and painting that has been interpreted as a visual symbol of a figure's possession of a particular insight or attribute. This can also be seen in the *himegami* owned by the Yamato Bunkakan, Nara, a mirror image of the Cleveland piece, and originally part of the same Usa Hachiman set. The Cleveland *himegami* portrays a young, relaxed woman whose features were sharply chiseled in a manner found in early tenth century sculpture.

The body is carved from a single block of yew, to which additions have been joined front and back with wooden pegs and metal tenons. The front horizontal piece of wood describing the crossed legs of the *hikogami*, is the only addition to that figure. It too is composed of yew, probably from the identical sacred tree felled for all five images, and all carved so that the wood grain runs in a basic vertical course.

Although this technical feature of the actual carving was never intended to be seen, to the modern eye it is appealing. Seen in conjunction with such deceptively simple carving suggesting monumentality and dignity, these *kami* typify the enduring character of Heian sculpture and of Shinto.—MRC

Published:
Etoh Shun, *Shinzō* (Tokyo, 1977), cat. nos. 3, 4.
Shimizu Zenzō, "Japanese Sculptures in America and Canada," *Ars Buddhica* 126 (September 1979): 72, figs. 19, 20.
Sasaki Kōzō, *Shinto no Bijutsu*, Nihon Bijutsu Zenshū, vol. 11 (Tokyo, 1979), fig. 51.
Kurata Bunsaku, ed., *Chōkoku*. Zaigai Nihon no Shihō, vol. 8 (Tokyo, 1980), no. 84.

7

## Guardian Figure

*Fujiwara Period, 11th century*
*Wood with traces of polychromy and* kirikane
*H. 93.2 cm.*
*Purchase, Leonard C. Hanna Jr. Bequest 69.126*

The figure is made from several blocks of wood joined together, the technique known as *yosegi* and characteristic of most wood sculpture from the eleventh century on. The joining, if skillfully designed and accomplished, prevented the splitting and checking that often occurred in single block sculpture (see cat. no. 4). The earlier guardian or warrior types are more massive and fearsome; this figure is taller in proportion than those and almost elegant in pose. Considerable remains of polychromy and cut gold-leaf patterns *(kirikane)* are to be found on the Chinese style armor. Originally, the figure must have held two attributes (sword? and spear?) whose handles would have passed through the holes in the hands. Like most sculpture of the Fujiwara period, following the mode introduced by Jōchō, the sculptor of the Byōdō-in at Uji (1053), this warrior echoes the aristocratic refinement and restraint characteristic of the last years of the Heian period.

The identification of the image is problematical. If the more curvilinearly carved demon curled-up beneath the warrior belongs to him (the demon is certainly about as old as the main figure), then the most likely identification is that of *Zōchō-ten* (*Virudakha*, or mighty) one of the Guardians of the Four Directions (in this instance South) placed at the corners of altars. The four guardian types are usually supported by demon-spirits. However, it is also possible, if the demon is an addition, that the figure is one of *The Twelve Generals (Jūni Shinshō)* of *Yakushi*, usually shown standing on a rock-like base.—SEL

Published:
Shimizu Zenzō, "Japanese Sculptures in America and Canada," *Ars Buddhica* 126 (September 1979): 70, fig. 11.

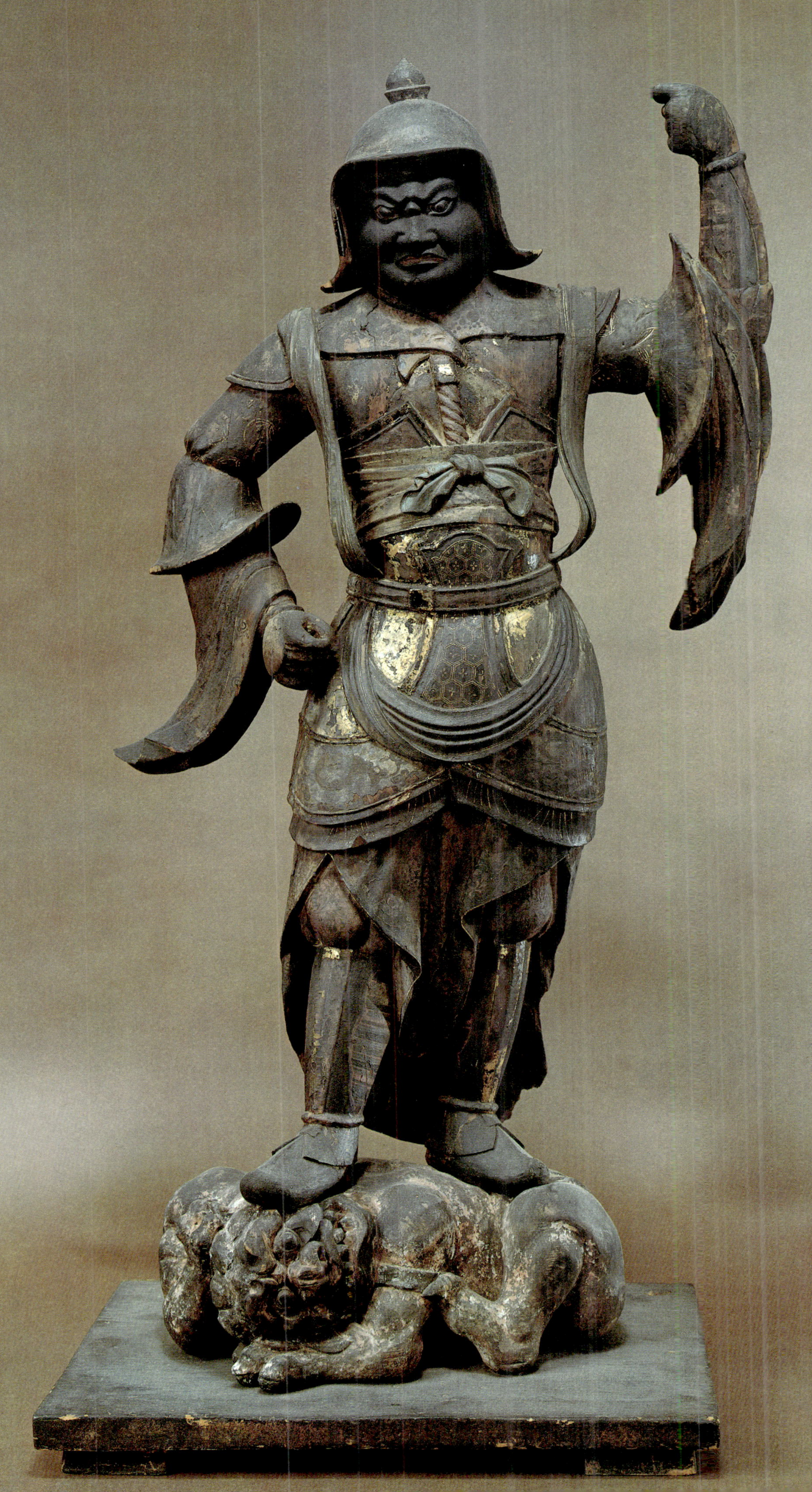

8

## Processional Mask of a Bosatsu

*Fujiwara Period, late 12th century*
*Wood with lacquer and paint*
*H. 21.9 cm.*
*Purchase, John L. Severance Fund 50.581*

*Gigaku* (see cat. no. 3) and later *Bugaku* performances at court and the major Buddhist institutions of Nara began to languish after the eighth century and the move of the capital to Kyoto. In their stead a new kind of processional ceremony developed and gained favor during the tenth and eleventh centuries.

Known as "ceremony of welcoming" *(mukae-kō)* because of its subsequent association with the popular Pure Land sect beliefs of the later Heian and Kamakura periods, this procession originated in various ninth century religious rites celebrating the consecration of a new temple or the public unveiling of a secret image. In such instances the secret image was carried through the streets of Kyoto or Nara by attendants wearing masks in a procession called *neri-kuyō*. During the course of the procession religious events relating to the holy image would be enacted at specific locations to the accompaniment of prayer, chant, and music.

This *gyōdō* mask represents a *bosatsu* (bodhisattva), an enlightened being who foresakes final redemption so that he can save other mortals. The mask was worn during performances of the *raigō* ceremony of the Pure Land sect, which preached salvation through faith in Amida and birth in the Western Paradise. Magnificent representations of *raigō* scenes happily survive today in Japan, most notably at the Byōdō-in and at Mount Kōya. There the modern viewer—like the Heian period believers and later worshipers—can see the radiant figure of Amida seated amidst numerous attendants and *bosatsu*. The welcoming procession must have imitated such painted heavenly visions in lively, popular form.

The gracious compassion of the painted representations of *bosatsu* can be seen in the Cleveland mask. It is carved from a single piece of light wood which has been covered with successive layers of lacquer, paint, and gesso. Holes were drilled for the eyes, nostrils, eyelashes and in the earlobes. Details of mustache, hair, and highlighting around the pupils and lips were drawn with fine-line brush strokes. The colors of hair and crown have been differentiated, and small holes in the crown band suggest that at one time a metallic diadem or clusters of jewel-like ornaments were attached to the mask.

This is a feature which can be observed frequently in Japanese sculpture and other extant *bosatsu* masks, particularly since they comprised the most numerous *gyōdō* mask type used in the welcoming procession. Usually twenty-five *bosatsu* masks were employed for the occasion, accounting in part for the variety of expressions visible in their countenances. The circumstances of their manufacture in Nara and Kyoto at the various sculpture studios beginning in the eleventh century allow for stylistic comparison with other *gyōdō* masks, and with contemporary sculpture. This example shows stylistic and expressive affinities with a *bosatsu* mask dated 1102 from Hōryū-ji, and a group of *Bugaku* masks from the Tanukeyama Shrine in Nara dated 1085, and three *bosatsu* masks now in the Kōmyō-ji, Kyoto, but reputed to come from a set formerly owned by the Hōrin-ji, Nara.

On stylistic grounds the Kōmyō-ji masks are datable to the last quarter of the twelfth century—the beginning of the Kamakura period—and provide an appropriate *terminus ad quem* for the Cleveland *bosatsu* mask. The sculptural affinities this mask shares with the early work of the renowned sculptor Unkei (late 12th-early 13th century), seen in the exquisite *Dainichi Nyorai* at Enjō-ji, Nara, has been noted by John Rosenfield.—MRC


Published:

John M. Rosenfield, *Japanese Arts of the Heian Period* (New York, 1967), cat. no. 33.

Shimizu Zenzō, "Japanese Sculpture in America and Canada," *Ars Buddhica* 126 (September 1979): 74, fig. 27.

Kurata Bunsaku, ed., *Chōkoku*, Zaigai Nihon no Shihō, vol. 9 (Tokyo, 1980), no. 97.

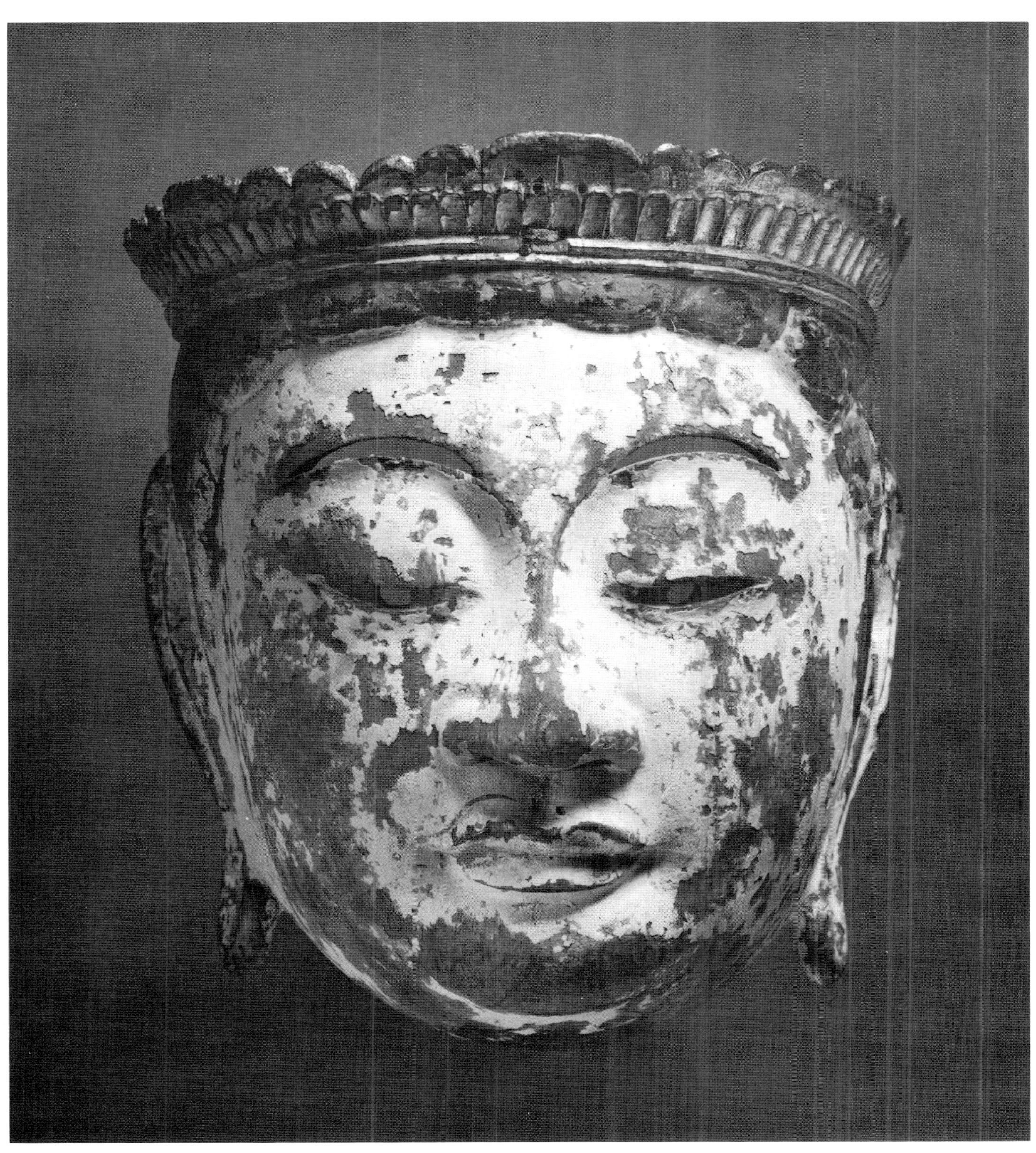

9

## Gohimitsu Bosatsu: "The Secret Five" Bodhisattva

*Kamakura Period, late 12th century*
*Hanging scroll; ink, color, gold, and silver on three joined pieces of silk*
*H. 79 cm. W. 63.8 cm.*
*Ex collections: Katano Satohiro, Tokyo; Masuda Tarō, Odawara*
*Purchase, Mr. and Mrs. William H. Marlatt Fund 61.423*

The Shingon and Tendai sects of esoteric Buddhism flourished during the Heian period. The founder of the Shingon sect was Kūkai, later known as Kōbō Daishi (774-835), who returned from China in 806 with the new belief that Buddhahood was attainable in one's present body. This promise was held out to the practitioners of the "True Word," directly transmitted from devotee to devotee. Kūkai placed great store in visual aids, diagrams or mandalas, devised to aid the understanding of difficult doctrine. Yet it was an essentially accommodating doctrine, aimed at resolving conflict through "non-differentiation of opposites." The Supreme Buddha was understood as the beginning and end, preceding and outlasting all things. All specific Buddhas and bodhisattvas were seen as emanations of the Supreme Buddha—a concept that could later be broadened to include Shinto spirits as well.

Kūkai is known to have returned from China with at least five T'ang portraits of the earlier (Indian) patriarchs of the Shingon sect (called Mantrayana in India, Chen-yen in China) and at least two important mandalas: the *Taizō-kai* (Garbhadhatu) with 407 deities in twelve sections representing the "womb circle" of principles and causes, and the *Kongō-kai* (Vajra-dhatu) with well over a thousand deities representing the "diamond circle" of reason and effect. The Supreme Buddha is at the center of both. The bodhisattva Vajrasattva occupied a special place in Shingon iconography, for it was believed that he had transmitted to the first patriarch of the sect the Supreme Buddha's "True Word" as relayed through the Buddha of the East. One of the various specialized mandalas derived from the *Taizō-kai* and *Kongō-kai* shows Vajrasattva as the "Secret Five" bodhisattva, *Gohimitsu Bosatsu*. Kūkai in 806 may well have brought a Chinese example of this particularly secret image to Japan along with the two master mandalas, for an eighth-century translation from Sanskrit already described it as depicting Vajrasattva surrounded by the following attributes: Desire (red and holding an arrow), Sense-Joy (white and emerging from the bodhisattva's right shoulder, one hand caressingly laid on the deity's chest), Passion (green, holding a beribboned staff with fish-like finial, ancient attribute of the Hindu god of love), and Anger-Pride (yellow, fists clenched)—four troublesome emanations of the Buddha-mind which, when understood, controlled, and channeled, led to enlightenment. The image holds a double five-pronged thunderbolt (vajra) in his left hand, in his right the vajra bell with which to awaken the faithful to wisdom.

Only five versions exist of this secret image. Among them, the Cleveland *Gohimitsu Bosatsu* ranks high in quality and earliest in date. Created in the late twelfth or early thirteenth century, the beginning of the Kamakura period, it still has the aristocratic and sensuous refinement—as well as theological complexity—of Heian art. It is geometric and starkly frontal, with a fire-whorl pattern in the halo symbolizing mystic energies, and the striking design and color chords confirm the early date of the icon. But the color, which in Heian painting was often carefully applied on both sides of the silk for rich and subtle effects, is applied here to the front only, and intricately cut gold-leaf patterns *(kirikane)* are sparingly used. The straightforward interpretation of this esoteric subject is in keeping with the development of Japanese art of the early Kamakura era.—SEL/UK

Published:
*Kokka,* no. 63 (December 1894), pl. 1.
Sherman E. Lee, "The Secret Five," *The Bulletin of The Cleveland Museum of Art* 49, no. 7 (1962): 158-166.
John M. Rosenfield and Elizabeth ten Grotenhuis, *Journey of the Three Jewels* (New York, 1979), cat. no. 17.

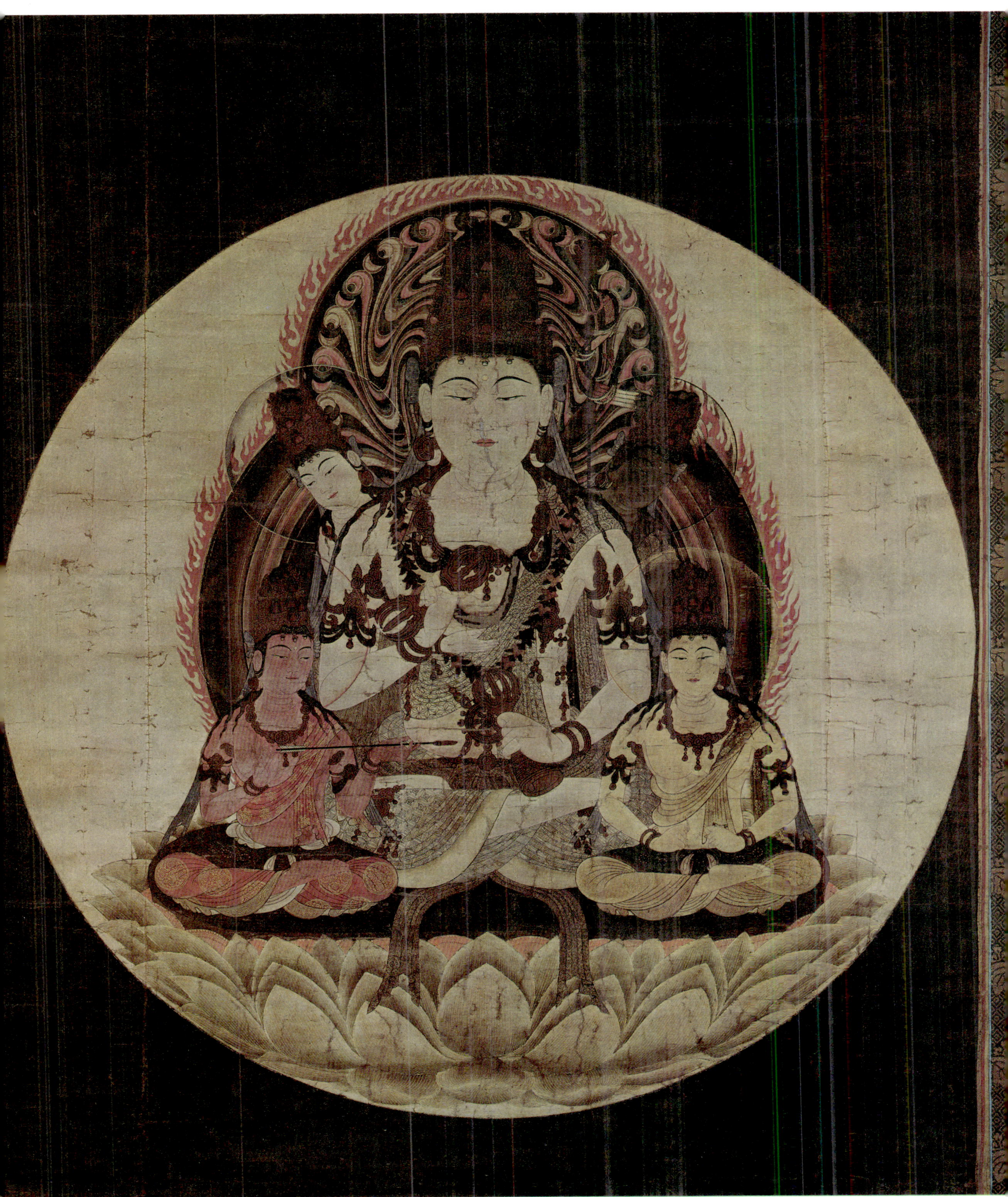

10

## Zaō Gongen

*Kamakura Period, 13th century*
*Wood*
*H. 106.7 cm.*
*Purchase from the J. H. Wade Fund 73.105*

Originally Zaō Gongen was a Shinto deity associated with Mount Kimpu in the Yoshino area south of Nara. He was adopted as a manifestation of Buddha types at the Buddhist temple of Ōmine in the mountain fastnesses of Nara prefecture. In this syncretic Buddhist-Shinto (see also cat. no. 15) practice during the Heian period, he was shown in an image type derived from the Five Mighty Bodhisattvas *(Godairiki Bosatsu)* of early Heian esoteric Buddhism. The dancing pose, flaring hair, fangs and fierce expression, animal skin skirt, and display of the Buddhist double lightning bolt became his characteristics. Small bronze images of Zaō Gongen became common in the mid-to-late Heian period, but large-scale wooden images are comparatively rare. Since the cult of Zaō Gongen was one of ascetic, mountain priests, the use of small portable images is understandable. The Museum also possesses an image of Enno Gyōja the arch typical mountain priest who witnessed the appearance of Zaō Gongen during meditation. Enno Gyōja's cult in turn displaced that of Zaō Gongen in late Kamakura. This sculpture of Enno Gyōja is not available to Japan House as it is on exhibition in Japan.

Most of the larger wooden images date from the late Heian and early Kamakura periods. This energetic sculpture is carved almost wholly from one block of wood, a conservative technique in harmony with the nature of the image. The style too is conservative in its taut surfaces and planes, recalling work of the Nara period and reminding us of the deliberate revival of eighth-century style at the beginning of the Kamakura period. The vigor of the strong lips and the awesome expression of the head are remarkable. Some traces of color remain on the draperies and animal skin skirt.—SEL

Published:

Ikawa Kazuko, "Statues of Zaō Gongen and Kongō Dōji," *Bijutsu Kenkyū* 252 (May 1967), pl. ICa.

Shimizu Zenzō, "Japanese Sculpture in America and Canada," *Ars Buddhica* 126 (September 1979), pt. 1, p. 73, fig. 22.

Kurata Bunsaku, ed., *Chōkoku,* Zaigai Nihon no Shihō, vol. 8 (Tokyo, 1980), no. 90.

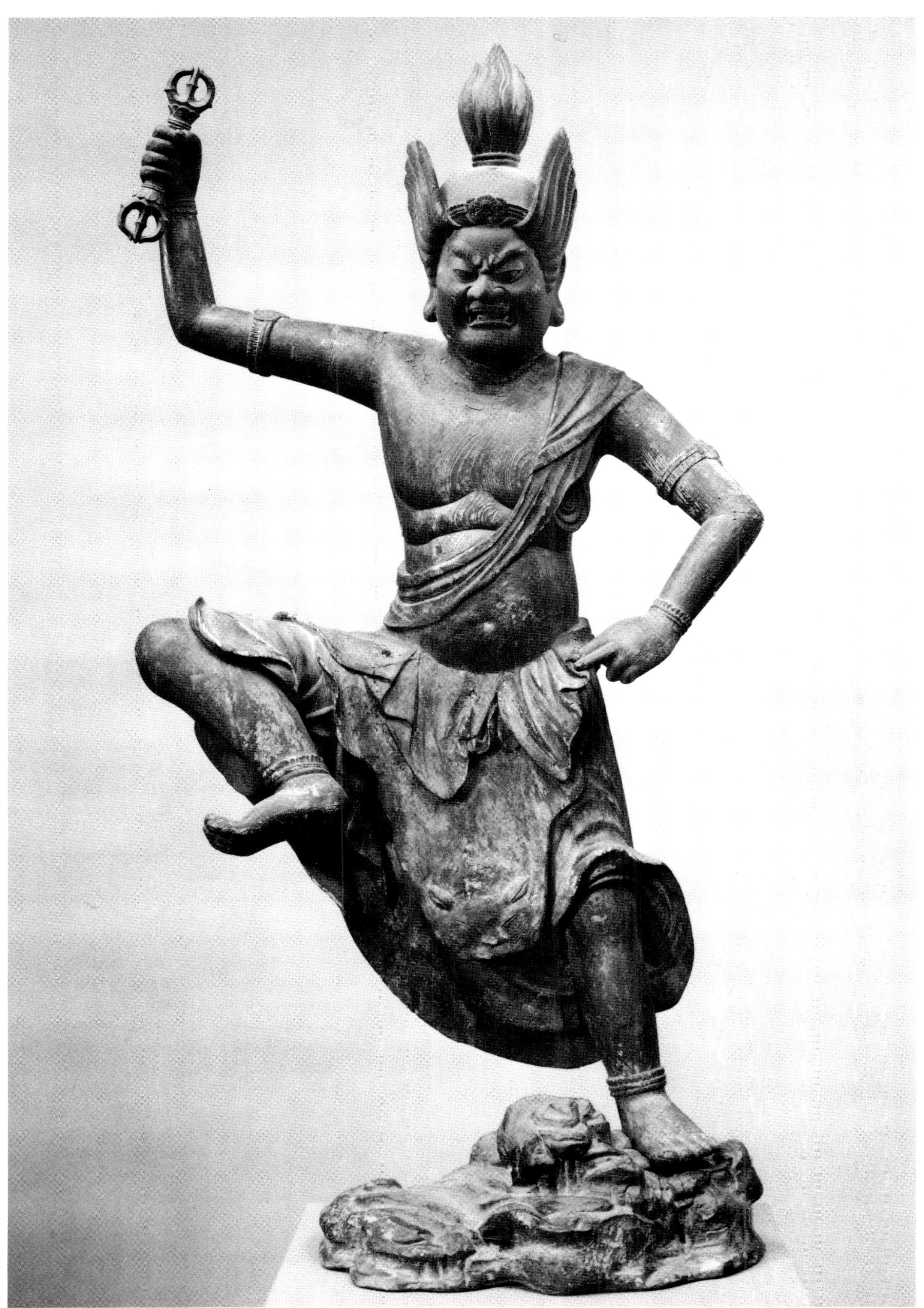

## 11
## Amida

*Kamakura Period, dated 1269*
*Kōshun, and assistants, Shinkō and Shin*
*Wood with* kirikane *and polychromy*
*H. 94.6 cm.*
*Provenance: Shitennō-ji, Osaka*
*Purchase, John L. Severance Fund 60.197*
*Detail illustrated on cover.*

If Shingon, "True Word," Buddhism was most completely expressed in the "womb-world" and "diamond-world" mandalas, the "Pure Land" teachings of the Tendai sect were based on the scriptures of the Lotus Sutra stressing the identity of the historic Buddha Shakyamuni with the eternal Buddha-nature latent in all beings and things. Both sects were brought from China to Japan at almost the same time, Shingon by Kūkai (Kōbō Daishi) in 806, Tendai in 802 by priest Saichō (Dengyō Daishi) who had studied at the sect's founding monastery on Mount T'ien-t'ai. Shingon with its complexities, elaborate rituals, and secret rites was the dominating force during the ninth and tenth centuries. Tendai demanded erudition and postulated the Supreme Buddha as the Absolute. In later Heian times, as a refined aristocracy expected art and life to be pleasing, the Tendai promise of direct rebirth into a "Pure Land" of unspeakable beauty competed successfully with the strenuous Shingon faith. Tendai also paved the way for popular movements in Buddhism during the Kamakura period. Among these, the Jōdō sect veneration of Amida, Buddha of the Western Paradise, became the predominant cult.

This golden image is a classic expression of the sculptural accomplishments of mid-Kamakura Amidism. This hollow and joined-wood sculpture carved with consumate skill, contained when it entered the Cleveland collection in its cavity three documents wrapped around a central wooden rod. These documents were a complete sutra confirming its identity as an Amida image; a list of donors indicating its original importance, for the names include two prominent priests of the time, one of them closely associated with the Pure Land sect and the other with imperial honors; and a dedicatory inscription signed by yet another renowned priest that records the date of the sculpture, the names of the artists—a master sculptor and two assistants, as was customary in the hereditary workshops so characteristic of Japan—and the temple for which the image was made. The information is translated:

> Principal sculptor, Kōshun. Assistant sculptors, Shinkō, Shin [signed] Joshun. The Buddha here is the one which was brought to the Yakushi-imu-[in?] no-dera of the Tennō-ji on the fifteenth of the fourth month. It was worked on since that date until the eighteenth of the fifth month when it was completed and dedicated. In order to complete it for the festival three people worked on it for five days at Yaoki village and then continued for thirty-three days at the Tennō-ji, beginning from the fifteenth day. Recorded on the eighteenth day, fifth month of the sixth year of Bunei [1269].

Despite the frontality and stillness of its stance, the figure has a commanding presence. The face is quietly serene; the robes have the wonderful flow of heavy silk and their folds deviate subtly from the general symmetry of their arrangement, avoiding static rigidity. The hands are held in the Amida *mudra* expressing welcome to the third grade of the "highest life." There is a crystal *urna* in the forehead and a pink jewel probably quartz in the hair. The eyes are inlaid with crystal from behind—a typical Kamakura touch that lends greater immediacy to the image. The Cleveland Amida combines Heian idealism and refinement with Kamakura realism—a precarious balance which later fourteenth-century religious art could rarely maintain.—SEL/UK

Published:
Sherman E. Lee, "The Divine and the Terrible," *The Bulletin of The Cleveland Museum of Art* 48, no. 1 (1961): 5-9.
Shimizu Zenzō, "Japanese Sculpture in America and Canada," *Ars Buddhica*, 126 (September 1979): pt. 1, 67-88, fig. 5.

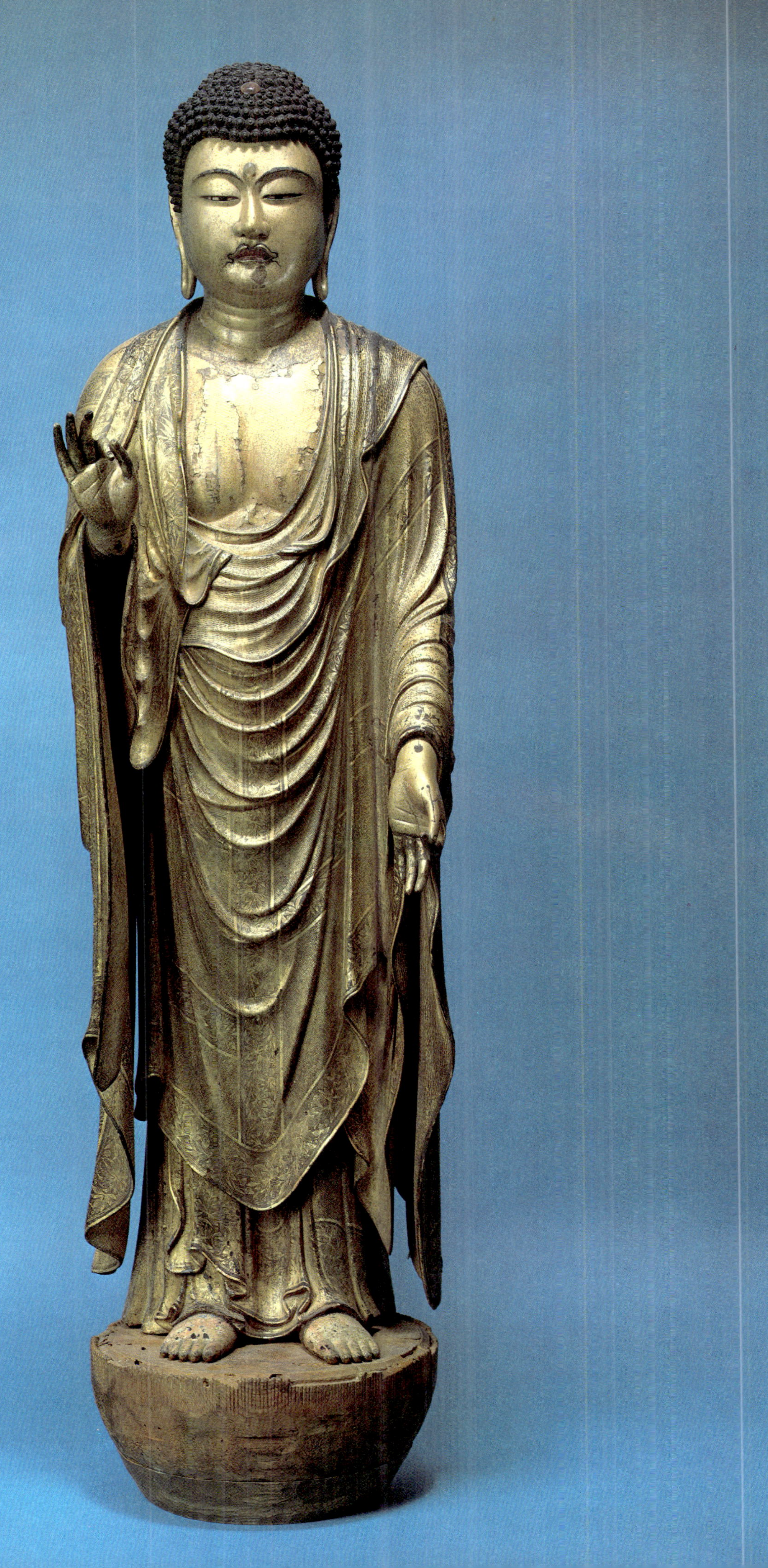

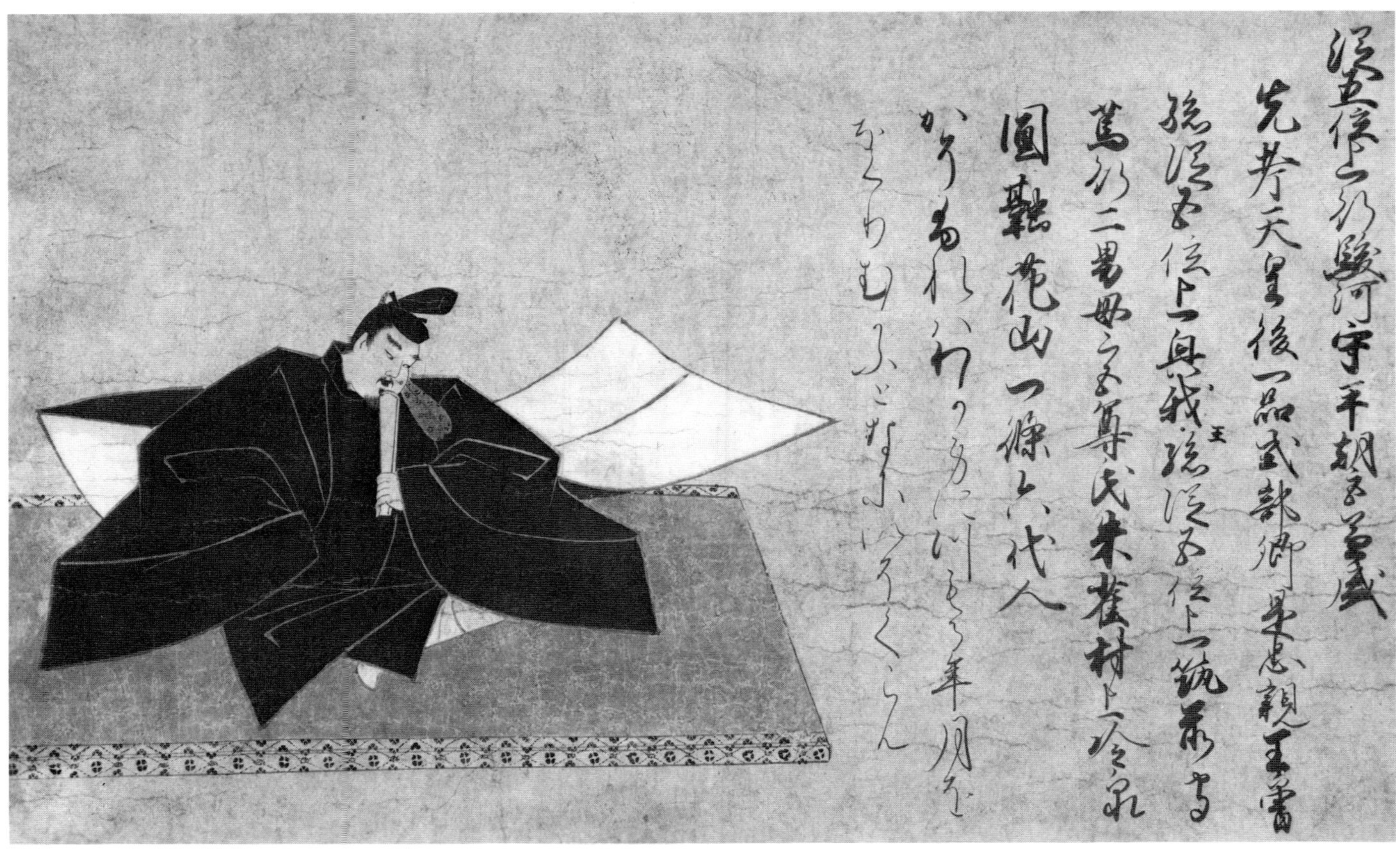

## 12
## The Poet Taira-no-Kanemori

*Kamakura Period, (1185-1333)*
*Section of a handscroll mounted as a hanging scroll; ink, white, and light color on paper*
*H.28.6 cm. W. 46.7 cm.*
*Ex collection: Inoue T., Tokyo*
*Purchase, John L. Severance Fund 51.397*

Taira-no-Kanemori was one of the "thirty-six immortal poets" of classical Japanese literature. He is depicted here, and to the right of the painting next to a terse biography of the poet is this poetic text: As I count, the years and months have piled on me. Why should anyone prepare for bidding farewell to one year and welcoming another? (trans. Tomita K.). The poets were an oft-repeated subject of Japanese scroll, screen, and album leaf paintings for the literate connoisseur. The identities of the chosen thirty-six poets were not necessarily always the same, and later paintings could include over a hundred famous poets of past and present whose inclusion varied with the taste of the times. Most of the portraits could only be ideal; Taira-no-Kanemori, for instance, died in 990.

The exchange of short poems on the mood of a poignant moment or the thrill of nature captured in verse was much in vogue at the Heian court (794-1185) as an intimate yet discreet form of communication. From ca. 1000 on, poetry and picture-painting contests provided entertainment at fashionable gatherings and the "thirty-six poets" became a favorite subject. However not until the Kamakura period does it seem to have been treated by professional artists.

The Cleveland painting is a fragment of what was once a handscroll depicting all thirty-six poets. Three other fragments of the same work (known as the Agedatami set), each showing a poet seated in stiffly starched court robes on a mat with textile borders, are now at the Freer Gallery in Washington. A total of twelve poets from the set are at present accounted for. This set and a similar, slightly earlier one, formerly in the Marquis Satake collection, have traditionally been attributed to Fujiwara-no-Nobuzane (1176-1265?) who is known to have painted the thirty-six poets in 1233. Nobuzane, a member of the Fujiwara clan and son of Takanobu, a courtier and poet with a gift for portrait painting, was a prominent court painter in the early Kamakura period who continued to paint in the decorative *Yamato-e* manner associated with the Heian court. He also carried on his father's tradition of portraiture and was one of the founders of the family guild that later became the court-oriented Tosa school of painting. The attribution of this painting to him is doubtful, but a close relationship to Nobuzane's original may well exist. Like the other fragments from the Agedatami set, the calligraphy is traditionally attributed to Fujiwara-no-Tameie.—SEL/UK


Published:

Shirahata Y., "On the Pictures of the Thirty-six Master Poets," *Kokka*, no. 721 (April 1952), pl. 3.

Sherman E. Lee, "The Poet Taira-no-Kanemori," *The Bulletin of The Cleveland Museum of Art* 40, no. 1 (1953): 7-9, illus. p. 11.

Shimada Shūjirō, ed., *Zaigai Hihō*, vol. 2 (Tokyo, 1969), p. 67, pl. 47.

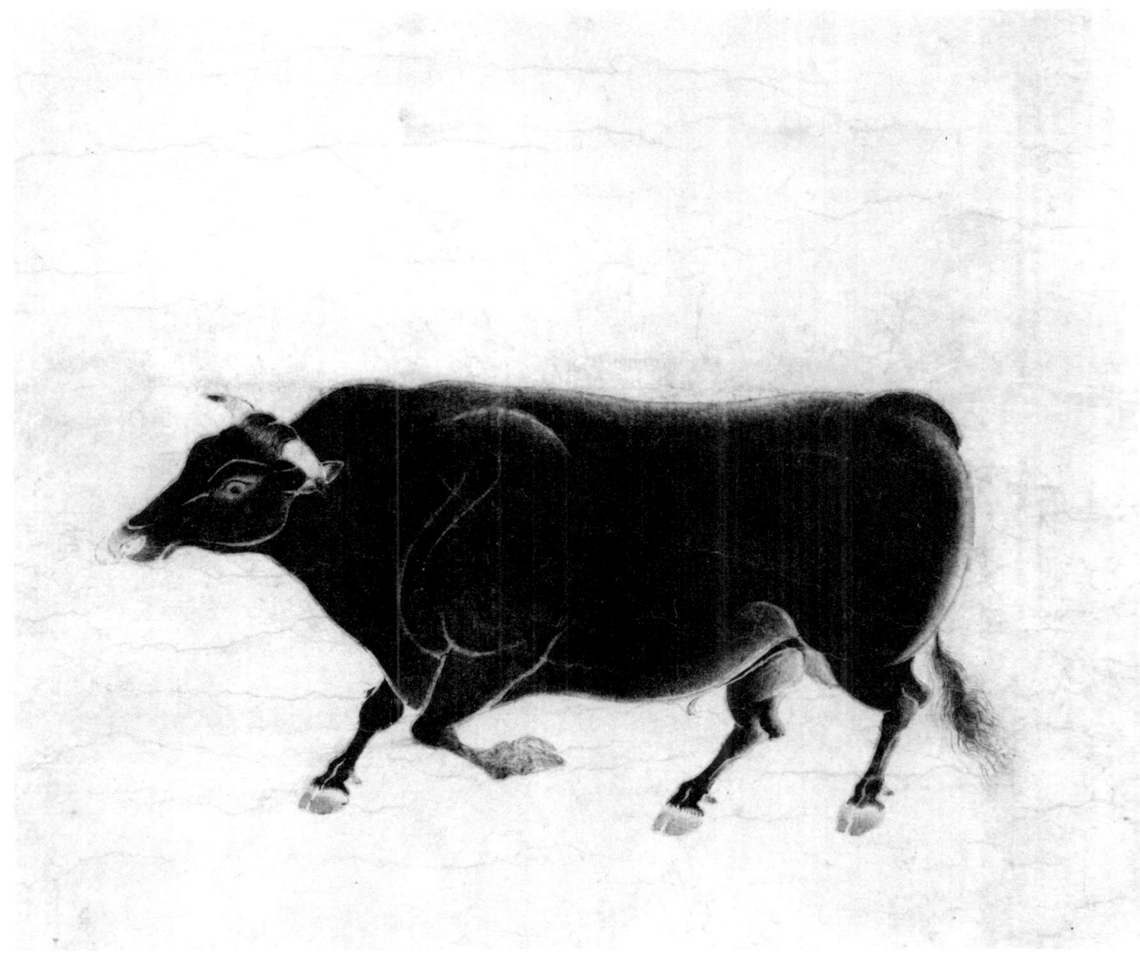

13

## One of the "Ten Fast Bulls"

*Kamakura Period, mid-13th century*
*Section of a handscroll mounted as a hanging scroll; ink and slight color on paper*
*H.27.3 cm. W. 32 cm.*
*Ex collection: Tanaka Shimbi, Tokyo*
*Purchase, John L. Severance Fund 52.286*

When the leading warrior hero Yoritomo of the powerful Minamoto clan assumed the title of shogun ("barbarian-quelling generalissimo") in 1185 and established a military government headquartered in Kamakura, political power shifted decisively from the imperial court and the aristocracy at Kyoto to the warrior class. The realism and directness of the Kamakura period (1185-1333) which reflected new attitudes to life, also found expression in painted and sculptured portraits and in the narratives of secular paintings.

The Cleveland painting of a bull, now mounted as a hanging scroll, was once part of a mid-thirteenth century handscroll portraying bulls from the ten provinces famed for producing the fastest and strongest beasts—a sympathetic samurai subject. The composition of the original scroll is known to us from surviving fragments and later copies. Cleveland's *Bull*, third of the ten, represents the breed from the province of Tamba, (west of Kyoto)—hard-hoofed, sharp-horned, slender-legged and irascible. Yet the realism of the forceful portrayal is highly selective. The massive black bulk has received but the faintest shading and the most subtle of linear emphases. The very essence of the animal is compressed into the simplified and tension-charged silhouette placed against a plain background. The temper and immense strength of the beast comes through large as life; yet we sense a decorative will at work in the placement of the silhouette, an impression confirmed by the detail of the gold-wash around the pupil of the bull's eye. Sōtatsu, Japan's greatest master of the decorative style in the seventeenth century, found inspiration for his own paintings on the subject in this Kamakura scroll of the "Ten Fast Bulls".
—SEL/UK

Published:
Sherman E. Lee, "One of the Ten Fast Bulls," *The Bulletin of The Cleveland Museum of Art* 40, no. 9 (1953): 199-200 illus. p. 197.
Mori Y., "Sungyū Zukan ni Tsuite" *Meihin Teichō,* ed. Ogushi M. (Tokyo, 1944), p. 97.
Michael Sullivan, *Chinese and Japanese Art,* The Book of Art 9 (New York, 1965), p. 116.
Shimada Shūjirō, ed., *Zaigai Hihō,* vol. 2 (Tokyo, 1969), p. 78, pl. 57.

## 14
## Nika Byakudō: The White Path to the Western Paradise Across Two Rivers

*Kamakura Period, ca. 1300*
*Hanging scroll; ink, gold and silver, and* kirikane *on silk*
*H. 123.5 cm. W. 50.7 cm.*
*Ex collection: Hara Tomitarō, Yokohama*
*Gift of the Norweb Foundation 55.44*

Contemplation of this hanging scroll of ca. 1300 and meditation on the parable it illustrates were meant to sustain the devotee's faith in Amida's saving grace on his perilous journey from the mortal world (seen in the lower half of the scroll) to the Pure Land of the Western Paradise (envisioned in the upper portion). The broad, vertically bisected band across the center of the scroll, decorated with a swirling flame pattern on the left (south) and torrential waves on the right (north), make it clear that the parable shown is that of *Nika Byakudō,* "The White Path Crossing Two Rivers." The parable originated in seventh century China and was often quoted by Hōnen (1133-1212), the founder of the "Pure Land" sect in Japan. The two rivers symbolize the destructive human compulsions of anger (fire) and avarice (water).

We see a man who, having left behind his comfortable daily routine (indicated by the flute and biwa players in the buildings at the bottom of the scroll), encounters killers and thieves, and the beasts, monsters, demons, and angry ghosts of the lower realms of "endlessly recurring existence" on his desolate journey west. Hoping to escape his pursuers, he reaches the shore of two raging rivers, a river of fire flowing south and one of water thundering north. It seems lethal to take the narrow white path between them, for flames and waves are furiously lapping across it from both sides. Equally certain of death whether he retreats or goes on, and despite the beckoning calls from his tormentors, the traveller decides to venture ahead. At this moment, the voice of Shakyamuni on the near shore praises his decision, assuring him that it will lead to his salvation, whereupon Amida enjoins him from the far shore to remain steadfast, so that the raging elements cannot harm him. The figure of the pilgrim in monk's garb occurs twice: confronted by the apparition of Shakyamuni as he comes running to the path, and again halfway across it. A small Amida triad waits in welcome on the far shore, Kannon proffering the lotus throne and Seishi seconding with prayer. Two arched bridges lead from the lotus pond up to the main platform where a second, and large Amida trinity is enthroned in majesty, Amida himself surrounded by a spoked, circular halo. Behind and symmetrically flanking the triad are celestial temples; along the top edge of the scroll appears a band of sky richly painted in powdered lapis lazuli or azurite, now darkened.

The deities are painted in gold, their robes delicately highlighted in cut gold-leaf patterns *(kirikane).* Before the gold became partially abraded or smudged and the silver darkened, this vision of paradise must have been a glowing one. The small mounds of land where the two little bridges rise from the lotus pond were painted in gold and silver, as were some architectural details ending with the finials atop the temples, all this contrasting with bright greens and orange as well as a deeper red. The treatment of the deities is somewhat soft and routine; their plump young faces seem idealized to a point of blandness when compared with the more vigorous and inventive treatment of the figures in the fire, water, and the mortal world. The fierce monsters, beasts, and men are drawn with zest—crisp and sharp, animated and realistic. The musicians in their houses and the horse trainer nearby provide a charming genre detail; the monk sitting in the graveyard near decomposing corpses and scattered skulls adds a coldly factual, somber note. Even the landscape with its subtle hues and the decorative trees in bloom seems more artful than the abstract splendor of the celestial region. This tension between the upper and lower portions of the scroll suggests that the painter might have been a professional secular painter trained in producing narrative picture scrolls (see cat. no. 24), rather than a Buddhist monk-painter specializing in hieratic religious imagery (see cat. no. 9).—SEL/UK

Published:

Sherman E. Lee, *Japanese Decorative Style* (Cleveland, 1961), cat. no. 19.

Shimada Shūjirō, ed., *Zaigai Hihō,* vol. 2 (Tokyo, 1969), no. 25, p. 39.

John M. Rosenfield and Elizabeth ten Grotenhuis, *Journey of the Three Jewels* (New York, 1979), cat. no. 37.

Hamada Takashi, et al., *Zaigai Bijutsu Kaiga,* Genshoku Nihon no Bijutsu, vol. 27 (Tokyo, 1980), pl. 15.

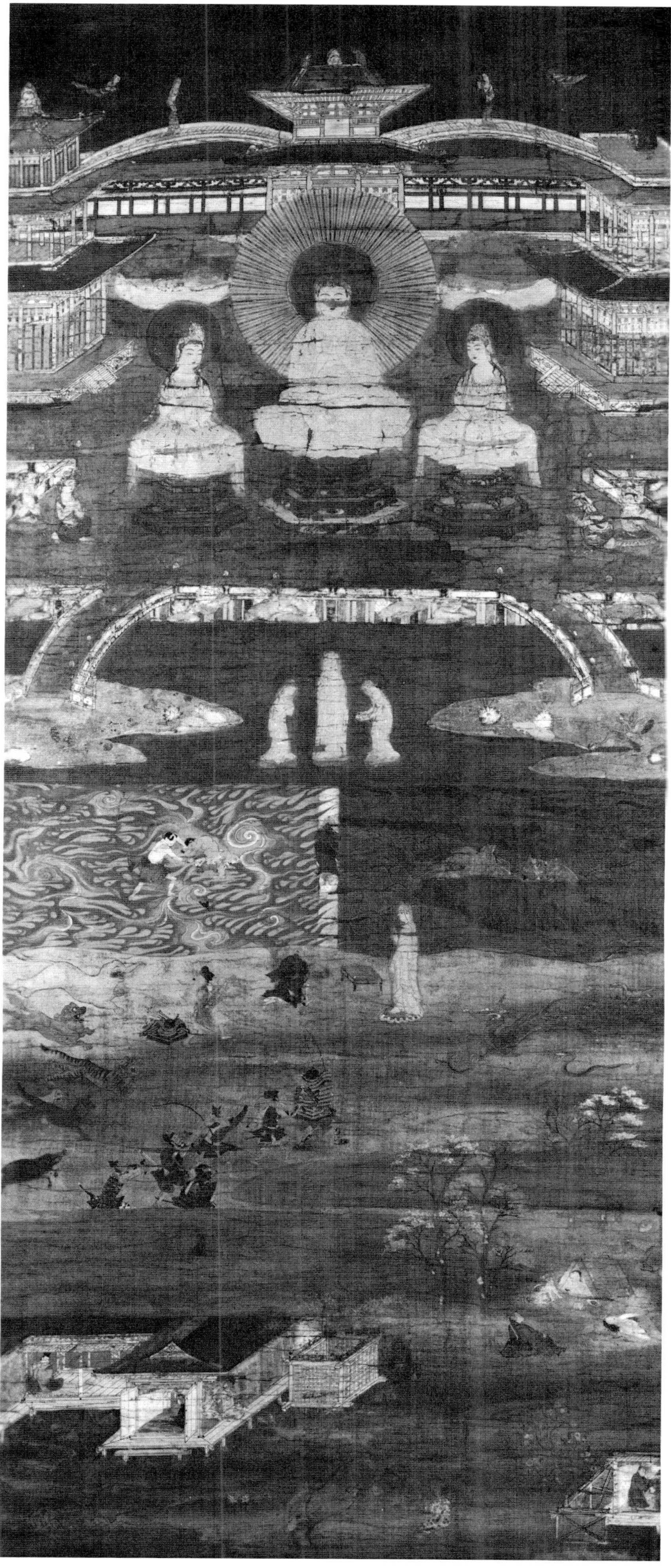

## 15
## Kumano Mandala: The Three Sacred Shrines

*Kamakura Period, ca. 1300*
*Hanging scroll; ink and color on silk*
*H. 134 cm. W. 62 cm.*
*Ex collection: Inoue Kaoru, Tokyo*
*Purchase, John L. Severance Fund 53.16*

While the most common Buddhist mandalas appear as geometrically structured schematic diagrams depicting major and minor deities placed according to their doctrinal functions, Shinto shrine mandalas often show specific Japanese temple sites in their landscape setting. Extant examples generally date from the fourteenth century or later; but the tilted ground plane permitting a sweeping "aerial" view, the informative topographic and architectural accuracy, and ubiquitous use of narrative figure painting derive from the earlier, popular Kamakura handscrolls illustrating the lives of priests and of miracles witnessed at certain shrines. On the other hand, the love of color and *kirikane* highlights, the bands of water and mist, the patterned undulations of hills played against quadrangles of red bark roofs in idiosyncratic perspective are conventions established by the sophisticated and decorative *Yamato-e* art of the Heian court. Unifying these two strains is the love of nature to be found in secular paintings of famous landmarks.

This Japanese love of nature, specifically the Japanese love for their native land, had found little opportunity for expression in the earlier Buddhist arts of Japan with their figural emphasis. Yet long before the introduction of Buddhism, such a relationship to nature had already been at the core of ancient Japan's indigenous religion, Shinto ("The Way of the Gods"), an undogmatic religion where all beings and things in nature were held to have their own *kami,* or spirit. Looming mountains or thundering waterfalls, as well as more modest natural sites, were revered as manifestations of deity, and pilgrimages were undertaken to shrines erected at such sites. Shinto beliefs remained rooted in the Japanese people as Buddhism spread from the ruling classes to the common people. Even the nobles continued their visits to the ancient shrines. Esoteric Buddhism eventually reconciled the two faiths: each Shinto *kami* could be understood as an emanation of the Supreme Buddha; Buddhas and bodhisattvas became tutelary deities of the Shinto shrines. Theological justification for this was advanced in the syncretic *(suijaku)* doctrine.

The Cleveland "Kumano Mandala" belongs to the syncretic type. The three Kumano shrines of old had remained fashionable during the Heian period, and the Kyoto court continued to make the often dangerous pilgrimage during the Kamakura era. As a devotional image, the mandala enabled the viewer to prepare for the trip, to recollect it or make it in mind only. To these ends, the painting had to be accurate, instructive, and vivid. A multitude of Buddhist deities hover within their haloes above the three shrines. The path leads from Hongū through Shingū to remote Nachi, the oldest shrine high in the mountains by the famous sacred waterfall. On his journey through the lovely countryside, the imaginary traveller meets woodcutters, fellow pilgrims, even the first of the Japanese mountain priests, Enno Gyoja who died in 701, attended by apprentice-demons. This abundance of narrative details invites leisurely attention.

The strong *Yamato-e* traits suggest that the mandala was painted for a conservative patron. Its color scheme still retains some kinship with the "blue, green and gold" courtly landscape paintings of T'ang China (618-907). Yet it dates from ca. 1300—a time when more progressive Kamakura artists began to emulate the Chinese monochrome ink style of the Sung and Yüan dynasties.—SEL/UK


Published:

Kondō Y., "On Kumano Mandala," *Kokka,* no. 708 (March, 1951), pl. 2.

Sherman E. Lee, "Kumano Mandala," *The Bulletin of The Cleveland Museum of Art,* 41 no. 6 (1954): 116-118, illus. pp. 113, 122.

________________, *Japanese Decorative Style* (Cleveland, 1961), cat. no. 30.

________________, "Contrasts in Chinese and Japanese Art," *Journal of Aesthetics and Art Criticism* (Fall, 1962), p. 8.

Sasaki Kōzō, "Some Problems on the General Construction of 'The Ippen-hijiri-e Owned by the Kankidō-ji and Its Painter'," *Kokka,* no. 912 (March, 1968), pl. 6.

Shimada Shūjirō, ed., *Zaigai Hihō,* vol. 2 (Tokyo, 1969), pl. 39.

Kyoto National Museum, *Kamigami no Bijutsu* (Kyoto, 1974), cat. no. 23.

Sasaki Kōzō, *Shinto Art,* Nihon Bijutsu Zenshu, vol. 11 (Tokyo, 1979), colopl. 161, fig. 136.

Hamada Takashi, et al., *Zaigai Bijutsu Kaiga,* Genshoku Nihon no Bijutsu, vol. 27 (Tokyo, 1980) pl. 14 (detail), fig. a.17.

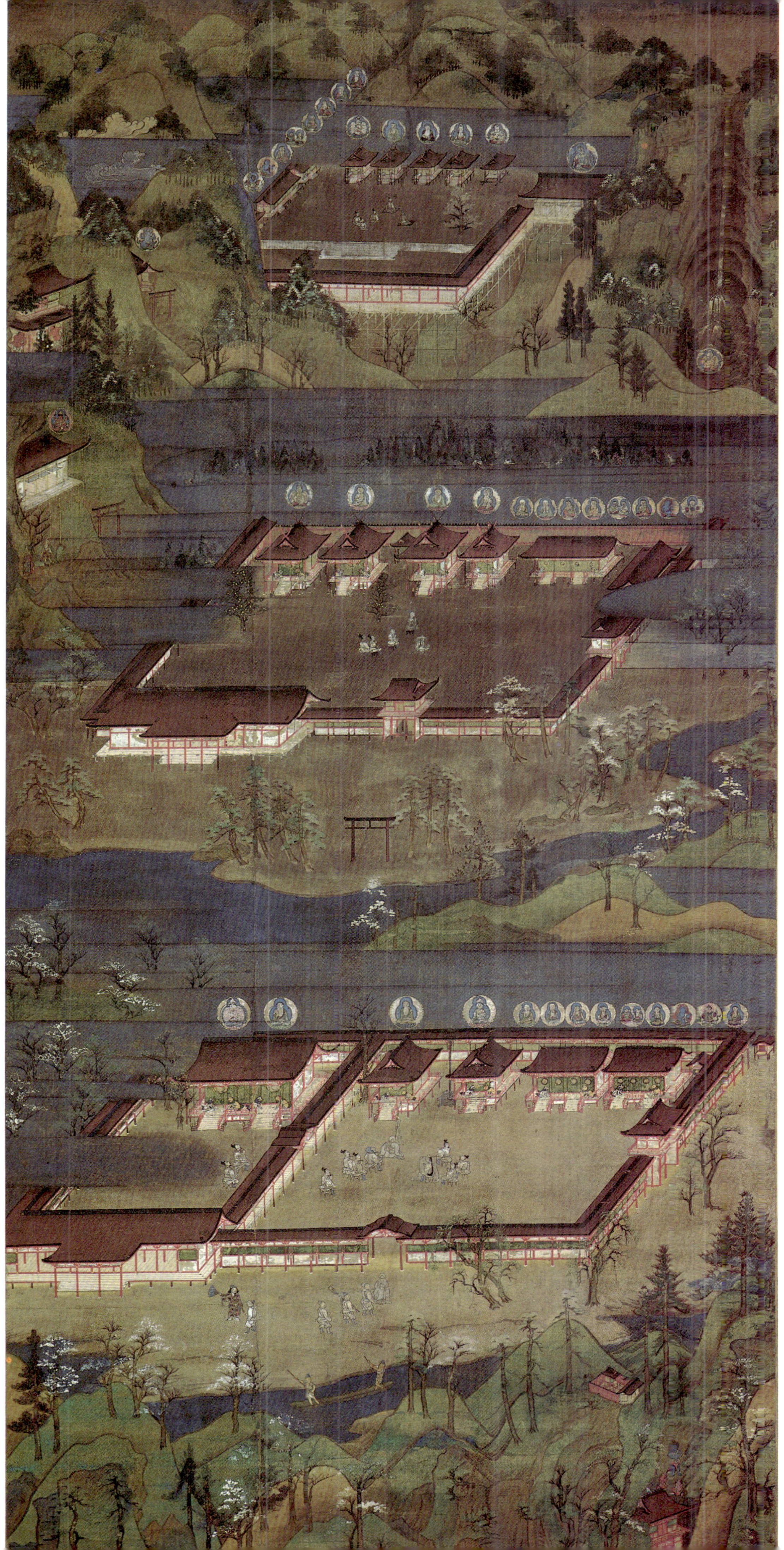

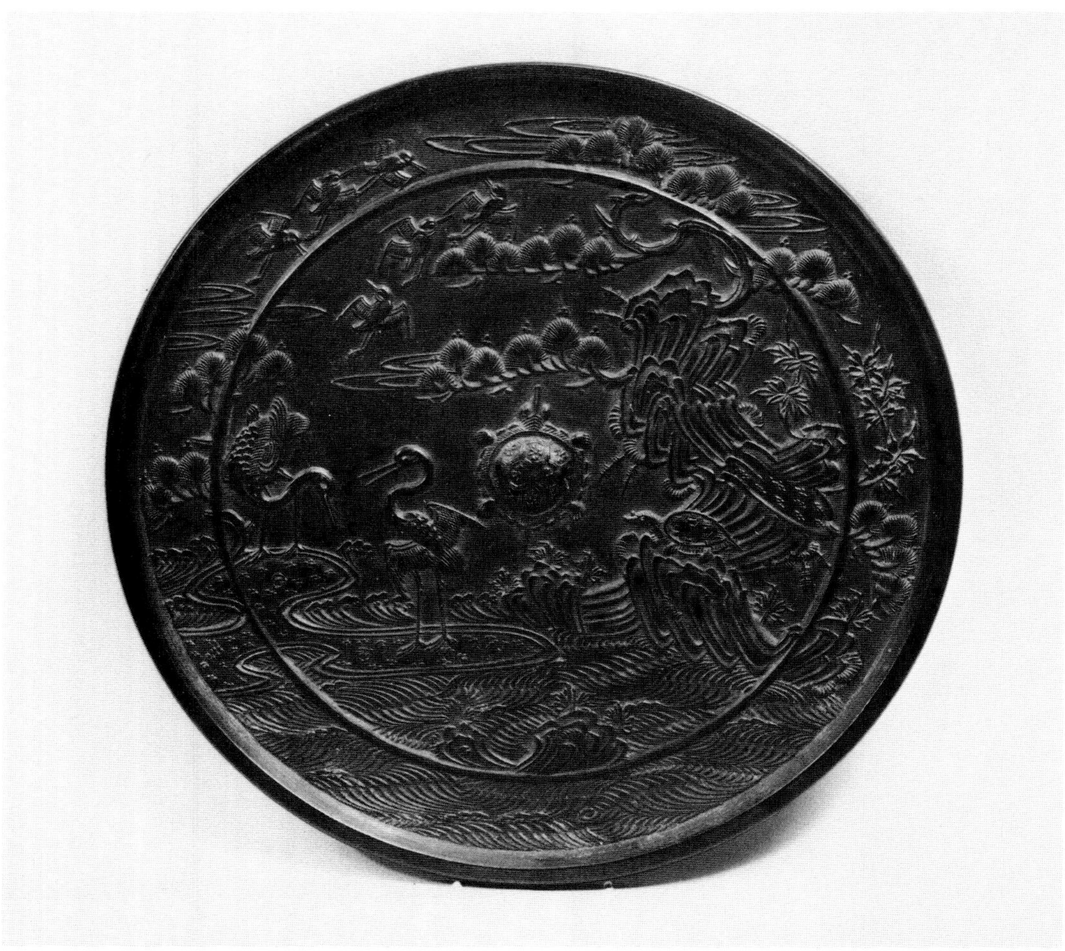

16

## Mirror with Island of Immortals

*Kamakura Period, 1185-1333*
*Bronze*
*Diam. 21.6 cm.*
*Purchase, John L. Severance Fund 70.65*

The mirror-back in the Far East, whether in China, Korea, or Japan, was one of the most fertile grounds for decorative and symbolic imagination. Mirrors were usually buried with the dead, either as symbolic accompaniments to the next world or as furniture used by the deceased owner and sent with him on his final journey. There are numerous examples extant, and many collections of mirrors have been made by collectors in all of the Far East. Usually the mirror, as befits a sun symbol, was circular, though square and oblate examples are not uncommon. The polished fronts provided the reflective surface, but the mirror backs were grounds for pictorial invention.

Again, the Chinese come first with a few examples recorded from Shang burials of ca. 1100 B.C. and increasingly numerous ones in Middle and Late Chou (9th-3rd centuries B.C.), Han (206 B.C.-221 A.D.) and later. The earliest Japanese mirrors of the Tumulus period (200-552) are excellent reflections of Chinese originals, with which they occasionally are found. Large and sumptuous "silver bronze" mirrors of both Chinese and Japanese manufacture are found in the Shōsōin Imperial Treasury at Nara dating from 753. After that time the Chinese mirror becomes more utilitarian and decoratively debased. But Japanese mirror design flourished in the Heian and Kamakura periods with numerous and varied pictorial designs intimately related to the other decorative developments in painting, lacquer, and textiles. The motifs come from both observation and poetic literary images—plovers, half-wheels, rush fences, the immortal symbols of crane, turtle, pine, prunus, bamboo, etc.

The early Heian mirror backs are still balanced Chinese compositions, but by the Fujiwara period a totally Japanese artistic language was achieved and expressed in castings of varying degrees of perfection.

This mirror, dating from the Kamakura period, uses several standard motifs in a unified pictorial composition well accommodated to the circular format. The plover (see cat. no. 17) fly at the edges; pines and cranes with overtones of longevity and good fortune occupy the center; the rocky mountain island is identifiable as that assigned to the blessed Taoist immortals by the presence of a tortoise on its lower boundary; prunus and bamboo shyly appear at the right of the rocks, making up the "Three Friends" with the dominant pine. The central boss of the mirror back is in the form of a second and more formal tortoise with its hexagonally divided carapace, signalling the ancient lore of the mirror—the center represents the axis of the universe resting on the world tortoise. The rich design and crisp casting mark this mirror as a classic example of Kamakura metal technology.—SEL

Published:
Harold P. Stern, *Birds, Beasts, Blossoms, and Bugs: The Nature of Japan* (New York, 1976), cat. no. 8.

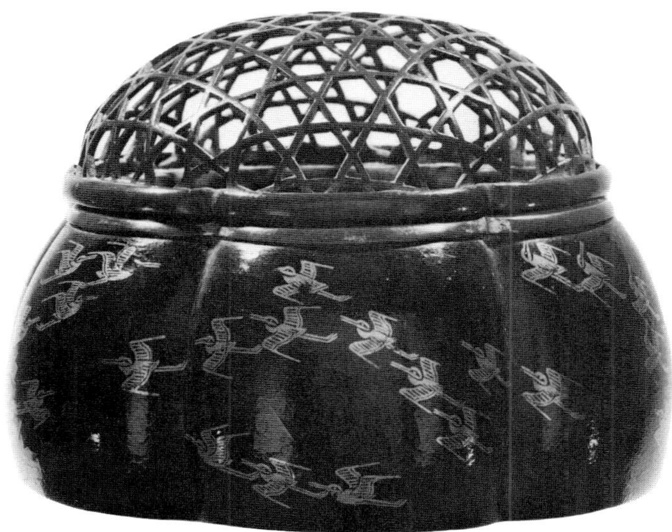

17
## Incense Burner with Plovers in Flight
*Kamakura Period, 1185-1333*
*Lacquer with gold lacquer decoration on wood, bronze cover*
*H. 7.6 cm. Diam. 10.8 cm.*
*Purchase from the J. H. Wade Fund 60.195*

While the melon shape of this lacquer utensil was new in the late Kamakura period, the decoration on the incense burner goes back to the poetry and designs of the Heian period. The small incense burner belongs to the new wave of Chinese influences in the thirteenth and fourteenth centuries and is related to, if not directly associated with, the more intimate scale of life associated with Zen Buddhism and ultimately the tea ceremony.

The technique of gold lacquer *(maki-e)* is a Japanese development of the Heian period, although it is present in rudimentary form on some of the T'ang style (or manufacture) sword scabbards in the Shōsōin Imperial Treasury given to the Tōdai-ji at Nara in 753 by the wife of Emperor Shōmu. Using sprinkled and brushed gold powder imbedded in dark brown or black lacquer, the Japanese artisan developed a wholly new and rich vocabulary of decorative and pictorial motifs to be used on carefully crafted boxes and containers for sutras, priest robes, cosmetic outfits, and general storage containers for fine things. Lacquerware became one of the most distinctive aspects of Japanese production in the useful arts. The variations possible with different shades and textures of both gold and silver, sometimes combined with mother-of-pearl or ivory, were seemingly endless but always controlled by Japanese sensibility and by images derived from past and present poetic literature. Thus, the origin of the present design, going back at least to Fujiwara lacquers, is most likely from an early tenth-century collection of poetry, the *Kokinshū,* where we find such poems:

In the Shio-no-yama (Mountain of Salt),
Along the thrusting seashore,
Sing the plovers
"The reign of my emperor
Will last forever and ever!"

The use of single-color gold for the design, as well as the single plover motif, indicate an early date for this example, probably within the fourteenth century. The shape is rare in any case, and only two others, both registered by the Japanese Cultural Properties Commission, are generally noted: the example with a design alluding to the *Genji Monogatari* at Tokei-ji, Kanagawa prefecture, dated to the early fifteenth century; and an example with flying birds and lattice design, at the Atami Museum, and described as from the Kamakura period.

The sprightly design of the flying plover was also used in the second flourishing of decorative style in the work of Sōtatsu, and especially Kenzan and Kōrin—notably in the well-known painted ceramic tray in the Cleveland collection, a collaborative work of both artists.—SEL

Published:
Sherman E. Lee, *Japanese Decorative Style* (Cleveland, 1961), cat. no. 37.

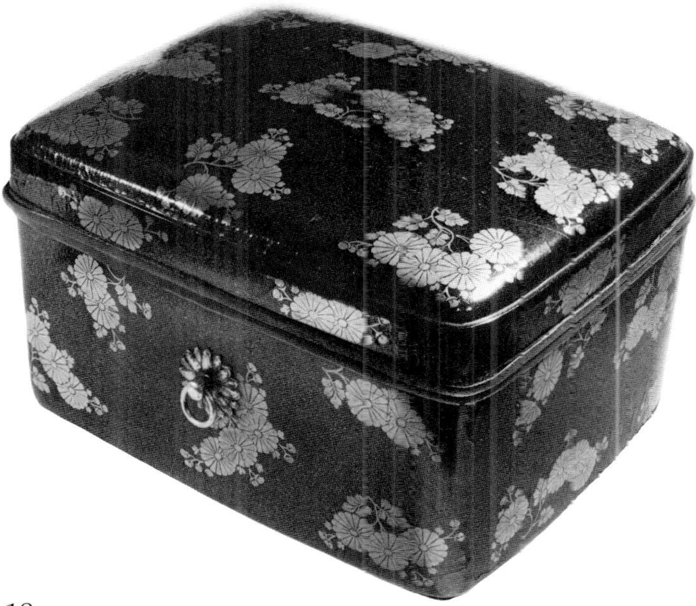

18
## Box with Chrysanthemum Design
*Kamakura Period, 1185-1333*
*Lacquer with flat gold decoration*
*H. 17.5 cm. W. 27.3 cm.*
*Purchase, John L. Severance Fund 63.513*

This lacquer box was probably used for secular material, possibly toilet articles. The deep brown lacquer is applied over a wooden core, and the background is filled with lightly sprinkled gold particles *(togidashi).* The rather carefully placed and somewhat symmetrical design of clustered chrysanthemum blossoms indicates a date in the late Kamakura period just after 1300, as do the swelling profiles of the lid and sides of the box. The gilt copper fittings (one a later replacement) are carefully adapted to the main decorative motif. The edges of the lid are bound, as is customary, with a pewter compound. A comparable box, particularly in the interior decoration of its lid, is in the Hatakeyama Museum, and is also dated to the late Kamakura period. At some later date, most likely in the seventeenth century, a sumptuous embroidered textile was used to reline the box. Early Japanese lacquer, that is, work produced before ca. 1400, is extremely rare.—SEL

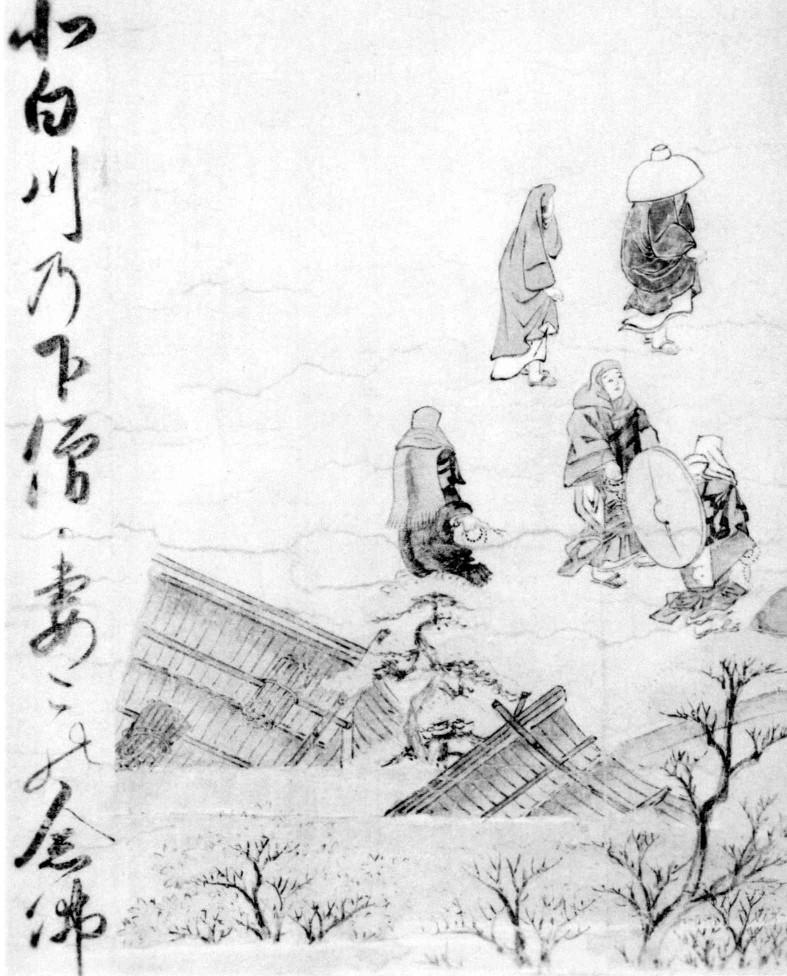

19
Yūzū Nembutsu Engi (Efficacy of Repeated Invocations to the Amida Buddha)
*Kamakura Period, 14th century*
*Handscroll; ink, color, and gold on paper*
*H. 30.3 W. 12m. 87.4 cm.*
*Purchase, Mr. and Mrs. William H. Marlatt Fund, John L. Severance Fund, and Edward L. Whittemore Fund 56.87*

From the late twelfth century on, the "Pure Land" teachings of the Jōdō sect centered on Amida's welcoming descent to fetch the pious souls of the dying into his realm—a subject joyously expressed in the arts and as fervently embraced by the common people as by the aristocracy. Picture scrolls taught the faith in easily understandable stories; the Amida name, Nembutsu, could be sung and danced to folk music. The later Kamakura period saw the rise of a new sect, Yūzū Nembutsu, according to which the mere repetition of the Nembutsu could gain admission for one into Paradise.

This is the second illustrated handscroll—the first is in the Art Institute of Chicago—of a set of two telling the story of Priest Ryōnin and the propagation of the Yūzū Nembutsu sect he had founded. The pair was painted in the fourteenth century and are the earliest of the known scrolls depicting this subject. In the Cleveland scroll, eleven sections of text alternate with fourteen scenes in ten pictorial sections in full color and gold. After a prelude in which even animals and birds plead for participation in the worship of Amida, the story begins with the death of Ryōnin and the air-borne descent of Amida's two golden emissaries, the bodhisattva Kannon offering a bejewelled lotus throne for Ryōnin's soul, followed by the prayerful Seishi, both crowned and haloed and arriving in an exuberant swirl of clouds and scarves. Other scenes show the transfigured Ryōnin appearing to a monk in his dream; a retired emperor-turned-priest and various court ladies joining in Nembutsu recitation rituals; a noble lady receiving the tonsure, her life in the nunnery, and her death; a peasant woman miraculously recovering from near-death in childbirth; and the release of a woman from the netherworld—all this due to the accumulated merit of Nembutsu recitation practice. The story of a country squire's family being spared from death during one of the frequent outbreaks of pestilence in medieval Japan includes a vision of ghosts, monsters, and demons from the lower realms of existence, painted with obvious gusto and appeal to popular fancy. The scroll concludes with a glorifi-

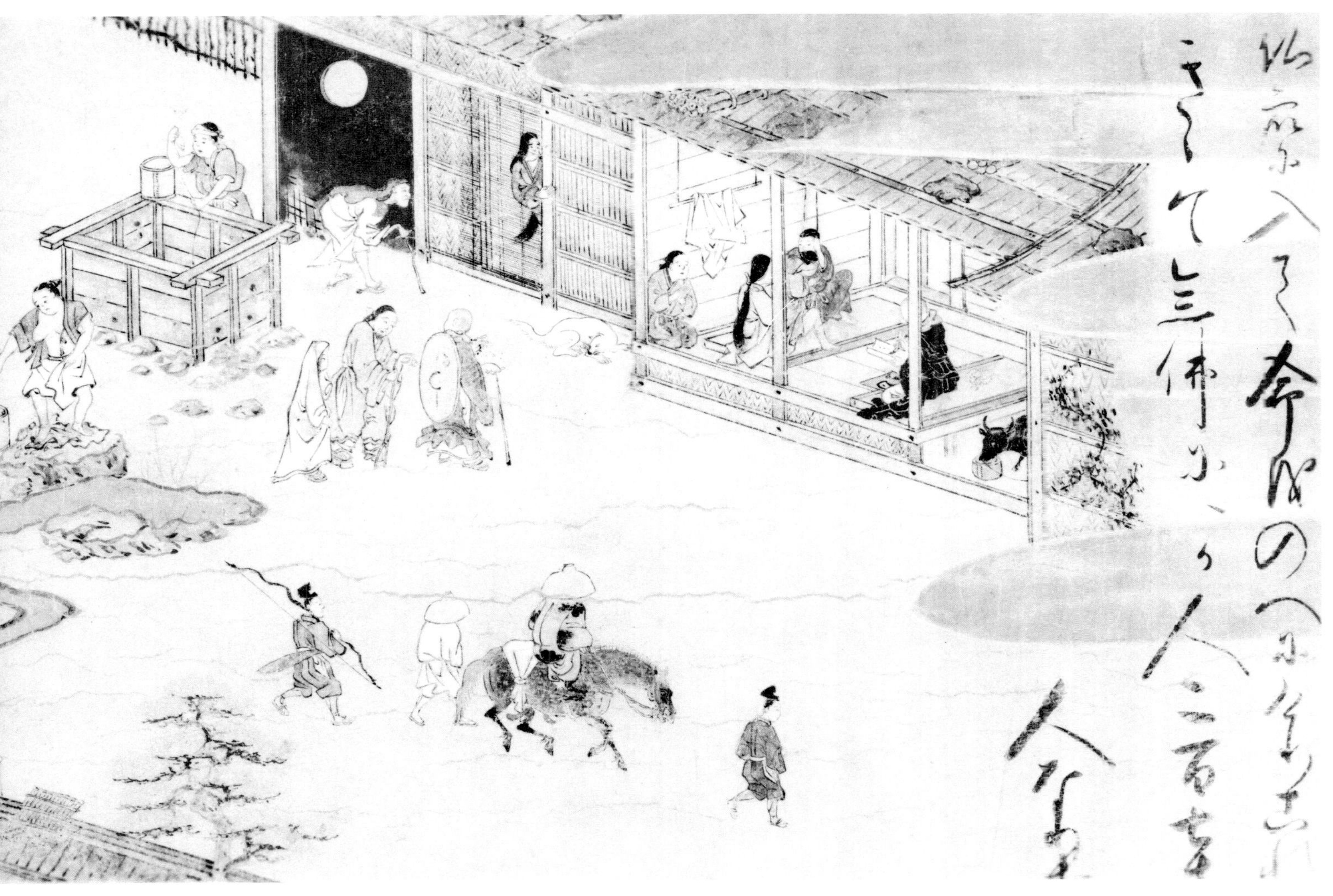

cation of Amida amid a mandala-like circle of faithful Nembutsu practitioners.

In the scene of Ryōnin's death, the celestial beauty and grace of the bodhisattvas contrast with the homespun reality of humble monks in their familiar surroundings—a dramatic clash of the real and the ideal. The sharp contrast in style serves the story excellently, but reveals how conventionalized Buddhist image types had become in Kamakura times, while secular themes were handled in a fresh and lively manner.

By 1100 a purely Japanese style emerged which could assert itself in secular art, unencumbered by Buddhist tradition. A distinctive national painting style evolved: *Yamato-e* (from Yamato, the old name for the Nara area, the nation's heartland, synonymous with "Japan"; and *-e*, picture). Drawing inspiration from Japanese poetry and romances, *Yamato-e* was originally created by and for a highly sophisticated court elite. Elegant and consciously decorative, the style is characterized by arresting color combinations, richly patterned costumes arbitrarily draped in flat, angular shapes, flat bands of low-lying mists winding across landscapes and interior settings which are seen as if roofless, the better to observe domestic scenes within an architectural framework of walls, partitions, windows, screens, and sliding doors in isometric-like perspective. The simpler tastes of the rising military class and even of the common people also found expression in scroll painting—in the narrative and naturalistic elements of handscrolls with a good popular story to tell.

The Cleveland "Yūzū Nembutsu" scroll has a few fine passages of *Yamato-e* style, especially in the courtly scenes. But its emphasis is on the narrative and on realism.—SEL/JK


Published:

Shimada Shūjirō, ed., *Zaigai Hihō*, vol. 2 (Tokyo, 1969), 83, pl. 60.

Tokyo National Museum, *Emaki Tokubetsuten* (Tokyo, 1974), no. 97.

John M. Rosenfield and Elizabeth ten Grotenhuis, *Journey of the Three Jewels* (New York, 1979), no. 40.

Hamada Takashi, et al., *Zaigai Bijutsu Kaiga*, Genshoku Nihon no Bijutsu, vol. 27 (Tokyo, 1980) pl. 31.

## 20
## Portrait of Hōtō Kokushi (Priest Kakushin)

*Kamakura Period, ca. 1286*
*Wood with traces of lacquer*
*H. 91.4 cm.*
*Provenance: Myōshin-ji, Wakayama prefecture*
*Purchase, Leonard C. Hanna Jr. Bequest 70.67*

The portrait sculpture of Hōtō Kokushi (1203-1295) of Myōshin-ji in Wakayama prefecture is carved in the *yosegi,* or "joined-block," technique which enabled the artist to handle the component parts separately. We sense his absorption in carving the face, his reverence for the priest becoming palpable. The searching realism of the sculpture makes it an outstanding example of Kamakura portraiture.

Hōtō Kokushi, shown in the stillness of sustained meditation, belonged to the mainstream of Zen Buddhism, a sect founded in India in the sixth century with a wide following in China (where it was called Ch'an) long before itinerant priests introduced it to Japan where it became particularly powerful during the Muromachi period, well after Hōtō Kokushi's death. Shunning scriptural erudition and teaching instead disciplined, intuitive meditation as a means of achieving enlightment, Zen relied on direct personal transmission from patriarch and from enlightened teacher to worthy disciple; hence the need to hand down in portrait form the most telling character features of the "transmitters" and the practice for disciples to be sent their own way with a portrait of the master. Painted Chinese prototypes for sculptured portraits of Ch'an notables, no longer to be found in China, survive in Japan, and these inspired a veritable wave of painted and carved priest portraits particularly realistic in their appearance—the Japanese outdoing the Chinese in fierce particularization. The convention of Chinese robes has been preserved here, but the pose has changed and the realism of the portrayal has sharpened. This may well be because such wood sculptures do not depend solely on the Chinese tradition. Japanese priest portraits, whether painted or sculptured, have a tradition reaching back to the Nara period.—SEL/UK

Published:
Kuroda Osamu, *Kumano,* Hihō, vol. 9 (Tokyo, 1968): no. 64, illus. p. 60.
Sherman E. Lee, "Zen in Art: Art in Zen," *The Bulletin of The Cleveland Museum of Art* 59, no. 9 (1972): 250, figs. 9, 9a, 17.
Donald Jenkins, *Masterworks in Wood: China and Japan* (Portland, 1976), no. 44.
Shimizu Zenzō, "Japanese Sculptures in America and Canada," *Ars Buddhica,* 126 (September 1979), pt. 1, p. 73, fig. 24.

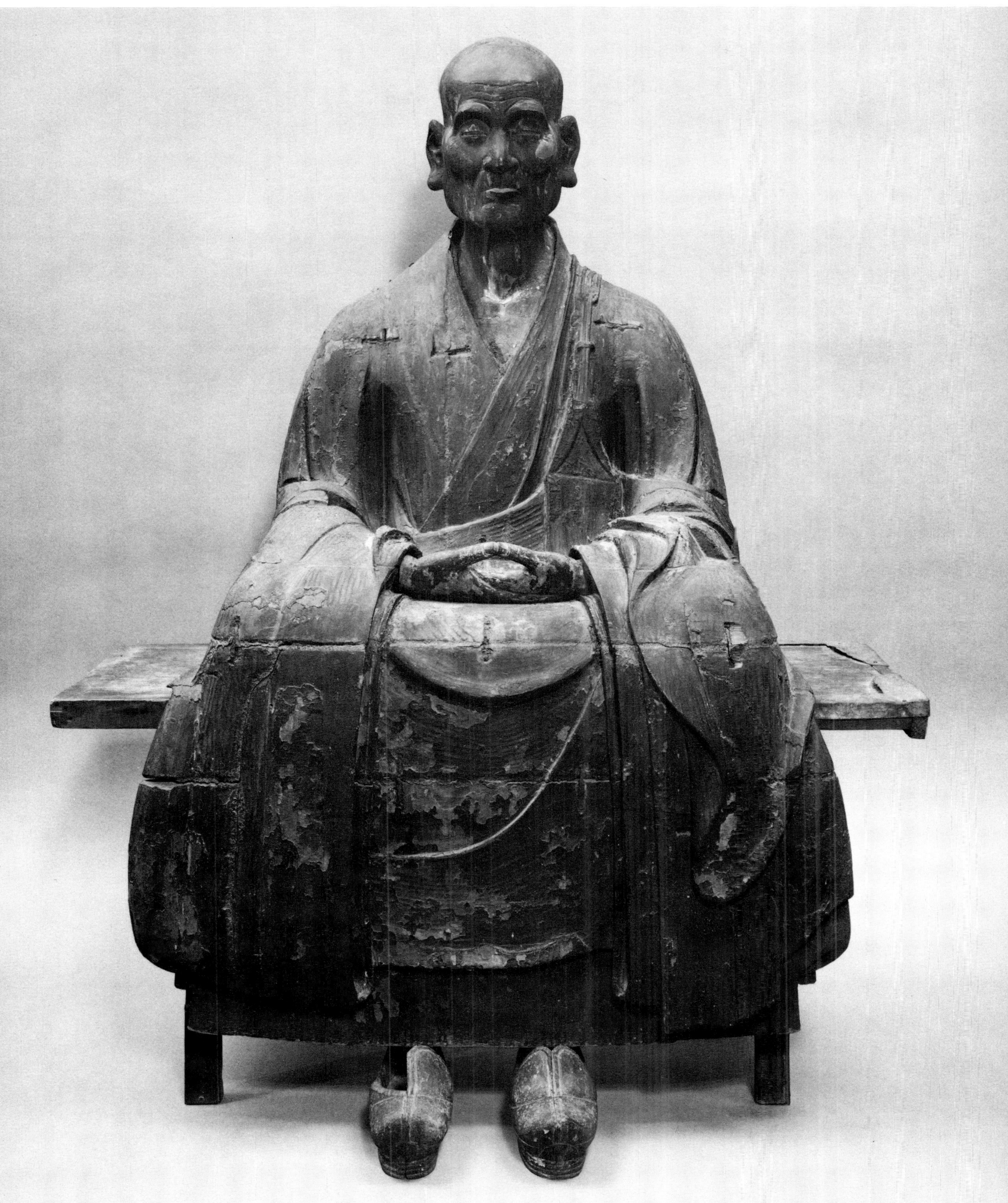

21

## White-Robed Kannon from Kōzan-ji

*Kamakura Period, ca. 1200*
*Hanging scroll; ink on paper*
*H. 91.5 cm. W. 45.1 cm.*
*Ex collections: Kōzan-ji, Kyoto; Hara R., Yokohama*
*Purchase, John L. Severance Fund 51.540*

Before the rise of Muromachi ink painting, there was an earlier monochrome discipline which served as an apprenticeship for the Japanese painter: the iconographic sketches of the esoteric Buddhist sects in the Heian and Kamakura periods. These sketches were models so the artist might fully master the necessary representations of a complex pantheon before setting his hand to color and gold on silk. They are characterized by powerful but even, descriptive black lines.

Kōzan-ji, a temple in northwest Kyoto, has a large treasury of works from the seventh century on. This includes a variety of sketches ranging from esoteric iconography through the famous "Frolicking Animals Scrolls" to an important group of at least four monochrome paintings which are the earliest representations of Zen Buddhist subjects in monochrome style. This painting is one of these four and has the seal *Kōzan-ji* stamped twice upon it.

The execution is free and easy. The brush was used with subtle flexibility, making lines thick and thin, wet and dry. Only essentials are stated and these are juxtaposed in a telling way—the smoothly falling, complex drapery against the large, rough form of rock. The quiet repose of the informally seated figure is supported by the large rock and punctuated by the smaller rock in the foreground, while the gently swirling lines of the water are minor echoes of the draperies.

The style is mixed. The dominant voice is that of China, in the draperies, face, and calligraphic brushwork of the rock. But curiously these last strokes follow a shape that recalls the rocks of an earlier Japanese style, as do the lines of the waves. Such a mixture is to be expected, for this is one of the first Zen monochrome pictures, a work of the thirteenth century, well before full establishment of the style and subject. The artist had certainly seen Chinese paintings of this Kannon, such as the famous Mu-ch'i triptych of Daitoku-ji. Between 1158 and ca. 1250 more than eighty priests went to China and returned, bringing back either painted or sculptured images in Sung dynasty style, such as the "Yang kuei-fei Kuan-yin" brought to Sennyū-ji by Tankai in 1228.

Kannon (Chinese Kuan-yin, who looks downward, hearing the sufferers; Sanskrit, Avalokiteśvara) is the principal bodhisattva of the faith—an interim mortal Buddha or "predestined Buddha-designate"—and as a masculine deity was variously represented in India from the first century and in the Far East from at least the fifth century. Kannon as the "Goddess of Mercy" is a later development and, all efforts to find an earlier origin to the contrary, was probably not represented before the tenth century. In her feminine form, white-robed and associated with the moon, water, lotus, and willow branch, she is a composite type as are so many popular deities. She is the merciful bodhisattva combined with some form of Chinese Mother Goddess, perhaps an earlier variant of the Taoist Maio-chen, a goddess associated with the sea (protecting seafarers) and babies (bestowing fertility). Kannon's attributes are those of mother images the world over: moon, water, branch, and hooded head. Her popularity was immense, and her images range from the most sophisticated products to penny broadsheets. Many Japanese paintings of the goddess exist, all deriving from such rare early prototypes as this fortunately preserved ink icon.—SEL

Published:

Sherman E. Lee, "A White-Robed Kwannon from Kōzan-ji," *The Bulletin of The Cleveland Museum of Art* 39, no. 10 (1952): 235-237, illus. on cover.

Wai-kam Ho, "Kaō: Myth and Speculations," *The Bulletin of The Cleveland Museum of Art* 50, no. 4 (1963): 77.

Shimada Shūjirō, ed., *Zaigai Hihō*, vol. 2 (Tokyo, 1969), p. 94.

Carla M. Zainie, "Ryōzen: From Ebusshi to Ink Painter," *Artibus Asiae* 40, no 2/3 (1978): 119, fig. 18.

Shimada Shūjirō, *Suibokuga*, Zaigai Nihon no Shihō, vol. 3 (Tokyo, 1979), 110, colorpl. 1.

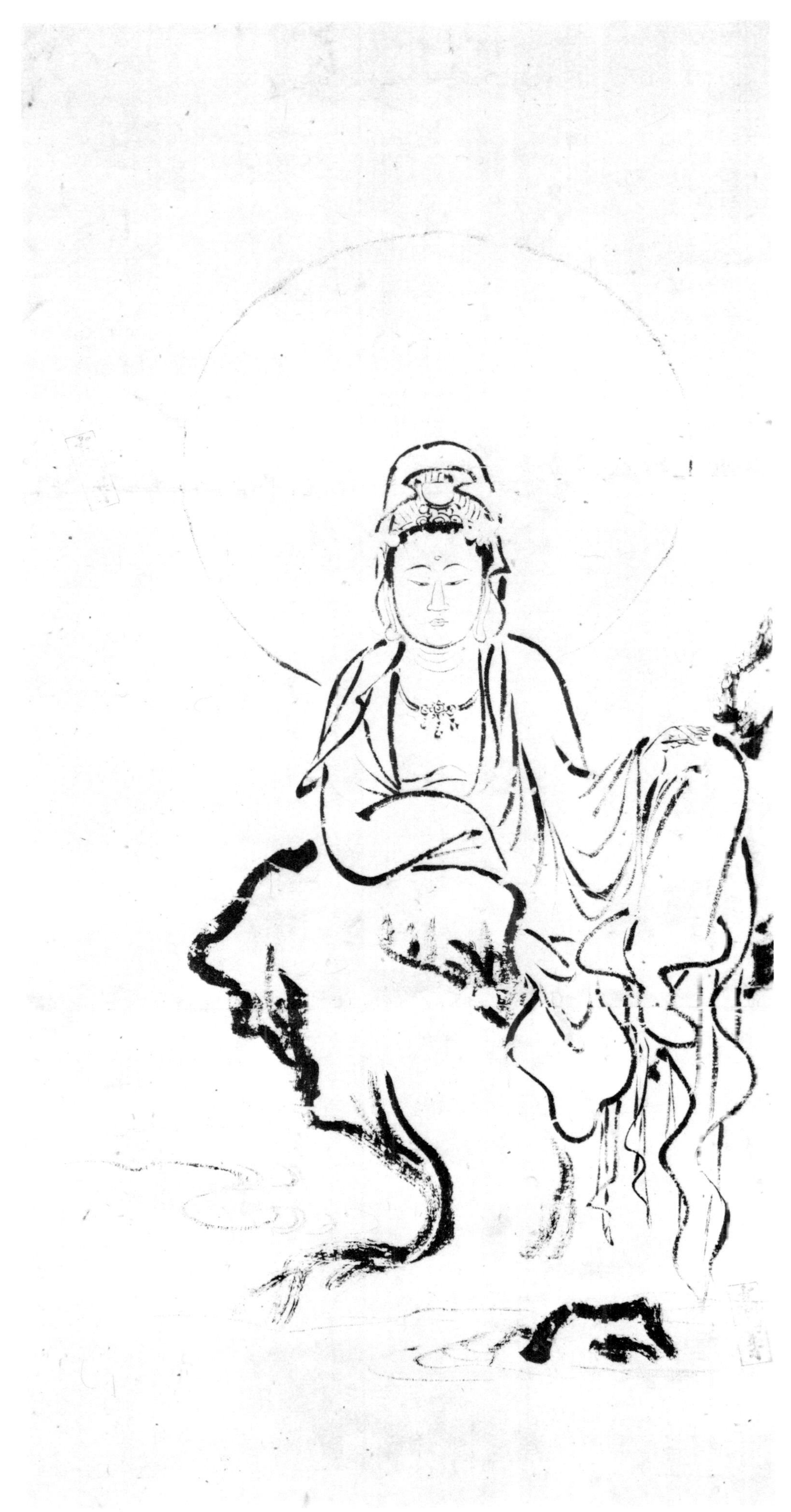

## 22
## Rock, Bamboo, and Orchids

*Bompō, 1348-ca. 1420.*
*Hanging scroll; ink on paper*
*H. 79.2 cm. W. 32.7 cm.*
*Purchase, John L. Severance Fund 72.15.*

In the spring of 1420, at the age of seventy-two, the monk-scholar Gyokuen Bompō abruptly left his residence at the Nanzen-ji temple in Kyoto and disappeared. Bompō had had a distinguished career, first as a young acolyte and functionary in Zen institutions in the capital and Kamakura, and then as abbot of temples in the western provinces. He returned to Kyoto when he was about sixty years old, becoming in succession abbot of two highly influential Zen temples: Kennin-ji and Nanzen-ji. During his tenure at the latter, he became a confidant of the fourth Muromachi period shogun, Ashikaga Yoshimochi (1386-1428), a great supporter of Zen culture in fifteenth-century Japan, a painter in his own right, and in all probability the man responsible for Bompō's departure from the capital.

Bompō was also an amateur painter, adept in the abbreviated brush manner associated with Zen painting since its introduction into Japan. His paintings, save one depicting bamboo, are all of orchids and rocks, a favorite subject in Japanese Zen circles. Earlier, in China, orchids and rocks had come to signify the rare literati-scholar or untainted government official. Paintings by both educated literati and Ch'an (Zen) monks frequently employed this visual metaphor for principled individuality in the face of foreign domination or excessive bureaucratic regimentation. The "Bamboo, Rocks, and Lonely Orchids" handscroll by the renowned Yüan literatus Chao Meng-fu (1199-1295) in the Cleveland collection represents this thematic and painterly tradition, as do orchid paintings by the monk-painter Hsüeh-ch'uang (P'u-ming; fl. mid-17th century).

P'u-ming's paintings were avidly collected in Japan, becoming models for later Japanese monk "amateurs:" The monks collected and studied such Chinese paintings, eventually affecting a stylistic transformation more compatible with Japanese taste. Bompō's paintings illustrate this process quite clearly and, moreover, indicate his determined efforts to accomplish an entirely personal development within this theme. Originally the convoluted rock from which the orchids, grasses, and bamboo in this painting issue was more centrally positioned on a ground that included tufts of grass and thorn sprigs. The ink technique features scrubby "flying-white" brushstrokes anchored by dark, textured dottings and generous ink swaths.

The orchid blades are executed in varied ink tonalities, forming deceptively simple arrangements of thin, twisting ink strokes across the painting surface. The sense of spatial depth which results, together with such elements as rock shape and rich ink expressiveness, helps place this scroll in a discreet stylistic group among the artist's twenty-odd known paintings. Examples in the Masaki, Asano, Fujii, and Metropolitan Museum collections echo the structure, ink painting techniques, and poetic sentiments of this Cleveland scroll.

Indeed, Bompō's position as one of the most admired literati of Kyoto is attested to by his numerous inscriptions on scrolls of poetry and painting by leading monk-painters of the capital of the early fifteenth century. These inscriptions, along with his orchid paintings and poetry, establish him as a prominent member of a small, influential group of monk-scholars active in the early Muromachi era. Prior to its acquisition by Cleveland, this painting by Bompō was virtually unknown, except for an Edo period copy of it and a record of its poetic inscription among Bompō's collected writings.—MRC

Published

Sherman E. Lee, "Zen in Art: Art in Zen" *The Bulletin of The Cleveland Museum of Art* 59, no. 9 (1972) pp. 238-259, figs. 13, 13a.

Shimada Shūjirō, *Suibokuga*, Zaigai Nihon no Shihō vol. 3 (Tokyo, 1979), pl. 16.

Hamada Takashi, et al, *Zaigai Bijutsu Kaiga*, Genshoku Nihon no Bijutsu, vol. 27 (Tokyo, 1980) pl. 42, p. 79.

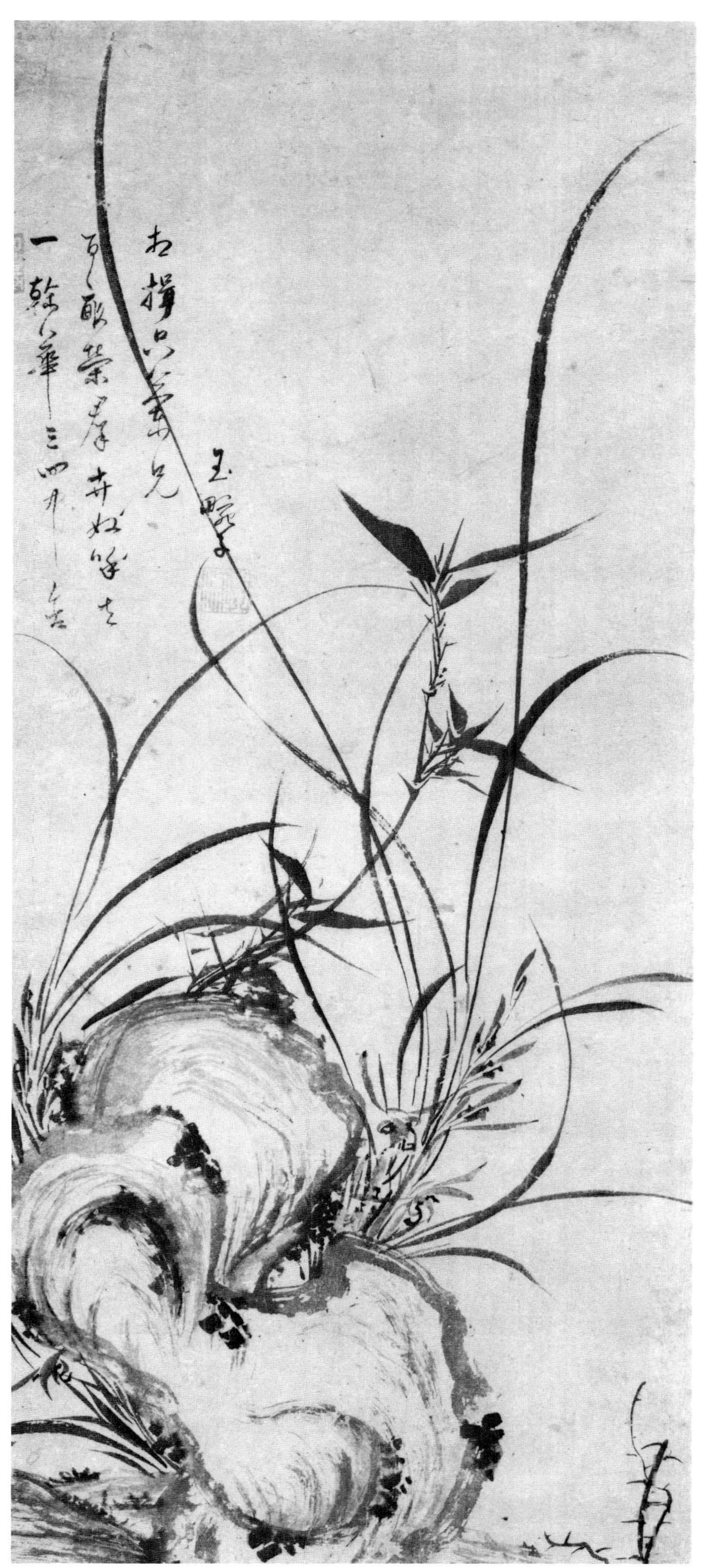

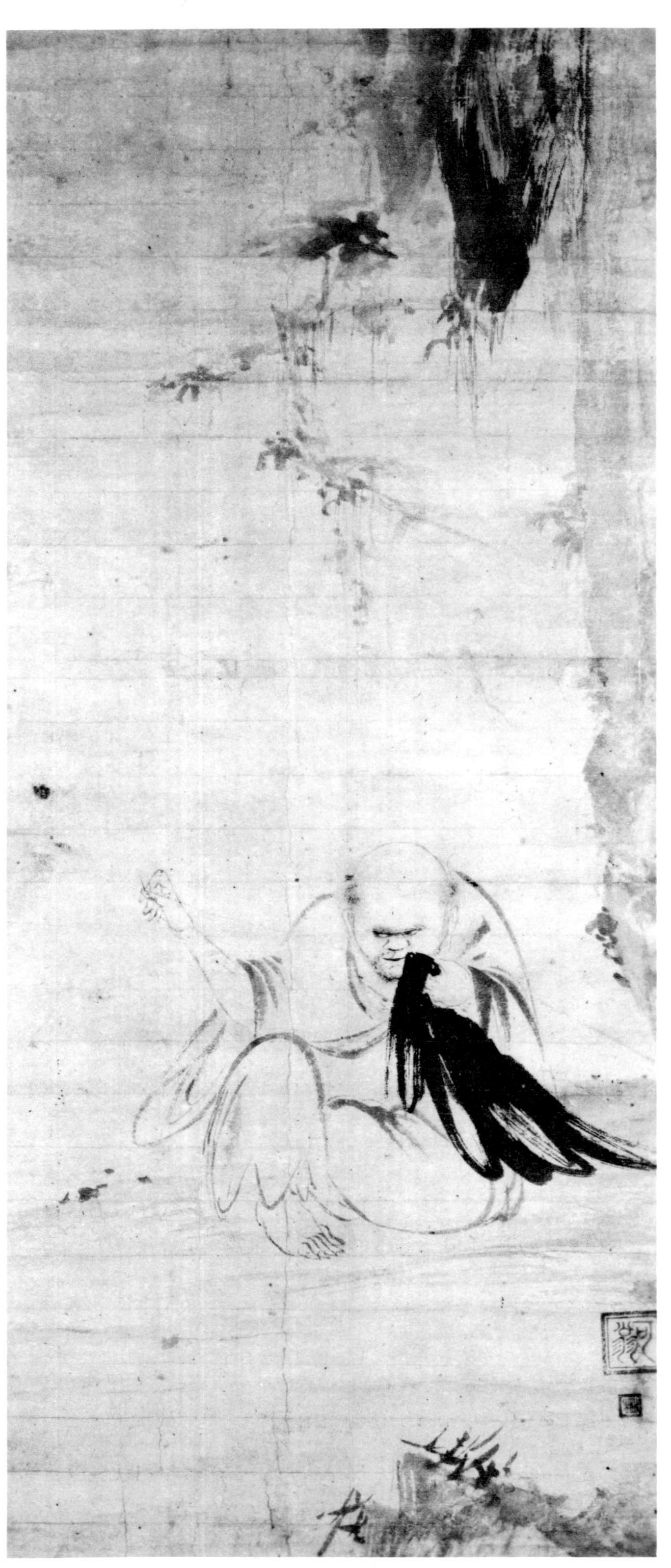

## 23

## Choyō: Priest Sewing in the Morning Sun

*Kaō; active ca. 1350*
*Hanging scroll; ink on paper*
*H. 83.5 cm. W. 34.7. cm.*
*2 seals: Kaō; Ninga.*
*Inscription partly erased over the seals: Seikai-jin hitsu.*
*Purchase, John L. Severance Fund 62.163*

It is easy to understand some of the reasons which encouraged the warrior class to embrace Zen Buddhism beginning in Kamakura times and especially throughout the troubled Muromachi era. Stern Zen teachers demanded discipline and unquestioning loyalty from their pupils as thoroughly as the warlords did from their vassals. At the same time, Zen taught the kind of self-improvement and stoic inner detachment from which the individual could draw the fortitude to comply with harsh duty. It is significant that Zen Buddhism depended heavily on intuitive understanding—a more rational, questioning attitude might have undermined compliance with the samurai code.

The Japanese admired the monochrome ink paintings of Sung China, whether of landscapes, birds and flowers, or figures—the latter often representing monks, hermits, or eccentrics unconcerned with the dictates of society. While the Chinese ink style was gradually developed and refined by a continuous line of master painters and was the product of a long tradition of high culture informed by Taoist and Confucian thought no less than Buddhism, Japanese emulation of Chinese ink painting was largely Zen-motivated. The Cleveland Museum's "Priest Sewing in the Morning Sun" combines with its pendant piece, "Priest Reading a Sutra in Moonlight," now in Boston, to illustrate the practical and spiritual rigors of Zen existence—self-sufficiency, humility, and religious training. The pair is attributed to the elusive Japanese monk Kaō of the mid-fourteenth century and derives from similar models ascribed to Mu-ch'i, the famous thirteenth-century Ch'an abbot and painter much admired by the Japanese. The priest mends his robe and stubbornly squints under the sun as he is about to cut the thread with his teeth. It is totally convincing, both as a work of art and a Zen exercise. The summary indication of a cliff along the painting's right edge and the overhanging gnarled root dripping with vegetation rendered in rich ink washes already give us a premonition of the magnificent landscapes in the "flung-ink" (*haboku*) manner by some of the later Muromachi painters.—UK

Published:
Osaka Municipal Art Museum, *Suibokuga* (Osaka, 1958),no. 40.
Wai-kam Ho, "Kaō: Myth and Speculations," *The Bulletin of The Cleveland Museum of Art* 50, no. 4 (1963): 71-79, figs. 1, 2.
Shimada Shūjirō, ed., *Zaigai Hihō,* vol. 2 (Tokyo, 1969),pl. 73.
Shimizu Yoshiaki and Carolyn Wheelwright, eds., *Japanese Ink Paintings* (Princeton, 1976), no. 1, pp. 42-47
Kanazawa Hiroshi, *Kaō, Minchō,* Nihon Bijutsu Kaiga Zenshū, vol. 1 (Tokyo, 1977), colorpl. 6.
Shimada Shūjirō, *Suibokuga,* Zaigai Nihon no Shihō, vol. 3 (Tokyo, 1979), p. 116, colorpl. 10.

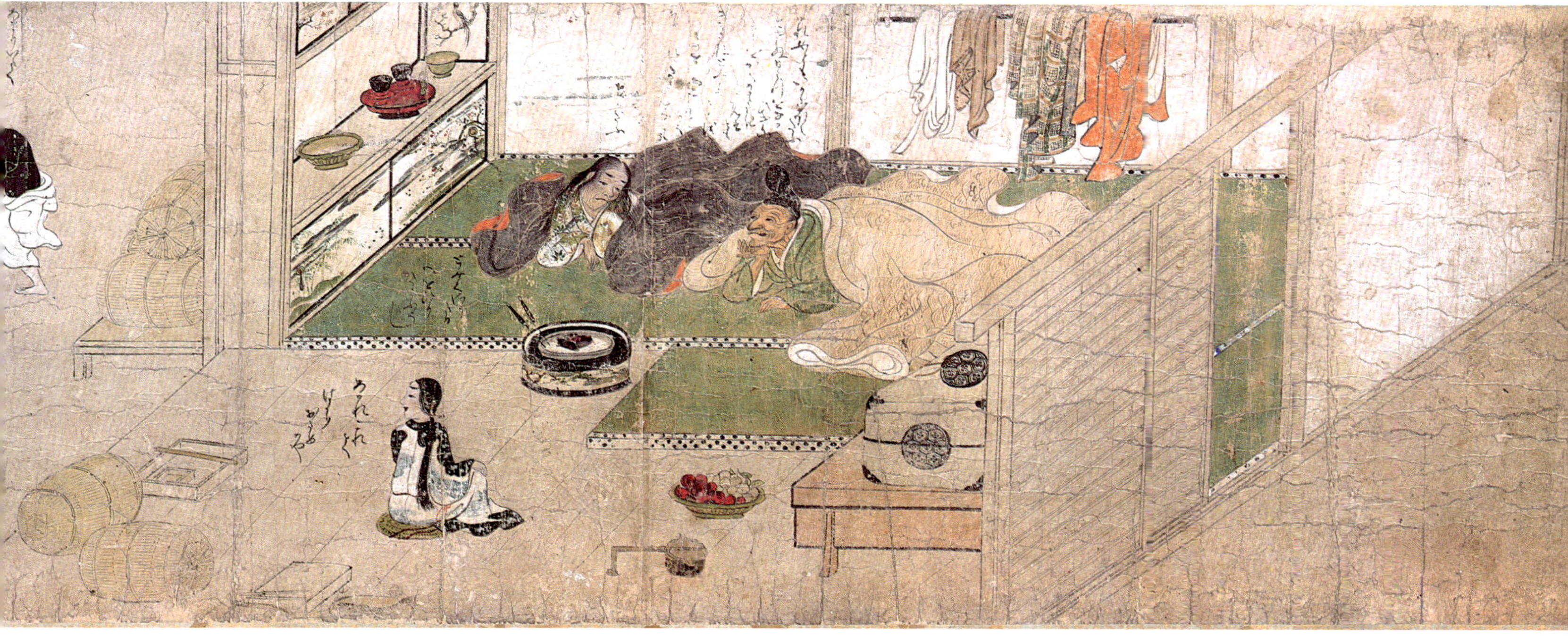

24
## Fukutomi Zōshi

*Kamakura Period, 14th century*
*Handscroll; ink and color on paper*
*H. 35.3 cm. L. 10 m. 28.8 cm.*
*Ex collection: Masuda Tarō, Odawara*
*Purchase, John L. Severance Fund 53.358*

The "Yūzū Nembutsu" handscroll (see cat. no. 19) is in the popular narrative style in which *Yamato-e* elements are used only when scenes of life at court appear in the narrative. The "Yūzū Nembutsu" scroll uses this style to spread the Amidist gospel, while more characteristic handscrolls are purely secular, such as this "Fukutomi Zōshi" scroll.

A narrative handscroll style developed in later Heian times, to become a major genre in the Kamakura period. While *Yamato-e* painters used literary sources of a distinctly aristocratic flavor, handscroll painters concentrated on folk tales and historical or religious narratives. If decorative splendor, refined static formality and restrained subtle indirection dictated by protocol are the hallmarks of *Yamato-e,* the narrative painters relied on fast-paced action, undisguised show of emotion, and pointed realism to hurry the narration along. Instead of the heavily colored, perfectly poised, doll-like figures of *Yamato-e,* these figures particularized almost to the point of caricature, are shown in vigorous motion and colored with washes thin enough not to obscure the swiftness of the outline drawing, thus enforcing the sense of movement. The format also attempts new compositional challenges. On long scrolls—the "Fukutomi Zōshi" measures over ten meters—a continuous story must unfold as each incident being unrolled already leads into the next. The same protagonist appears again and again as the scenes shift.

With unsqueamish realism, the scroll tells the mildly moralizing, naive, and hilariously gross story of a poor old man whose greed and gullibility caused him to cast common sense aside in the hope of turning his flatulence into a profitable performance, only to end up in shame. In the process, the viewer catches glimpses of village life: its beggars and poor, the courtier of rank with his ladies, servants, messengers, a nun, the neighbors, some old hags, the local doctor, and even dogs. It ends with two blind people pointing out to each other the object of derision. The actions and facial expressions of the seventy-seven figures in twelve scenes tell more than the accompanying text, often written in dialogue next to the corresponding speakers—a departure from previous handscroll practice and akin to the cartoon "bubbles" of today.

The Cleveland scroll tells only the second part of the story. The only complete two-scroll version survives in the Shumpō-in, sub-temple of the Myōshin-ji, Kyoto, and is in poor condition. The Cleveland handscroll painted in the fourteenth century, dates from the transition from Kamakura to Muromachi times; but the tale must have enjoyed enduring success, for it exists in several versions and seems to have been frequently illustrated during and after the Muromachi period as well.—UK


Published:
Shimada Shūjirō, ed., *Zaigai Hihō,* vol. 2 (Tokyo, 1969), p. 87.
Tokyo National Museum, *Emaki Tokubetsuten* (Tokyo, 1974), no. 41.
Akiyama Terukazu, ed., *Emakimono,* Zaigai Nihon no Shihō vol. 2, (Tokyo, 1980), no. 12.

25

## Horses and Grooms in the Stable

*Muromachi Period, 1392-1573*
*Pair of six-fold screens; ink and color on paper*
*H. 145.7 cm. W. 348.6 cm., each*
*Ex collections: Tokugawa, Shima*
*Purchase, Edward L. Whittemore Fund 34.373-.374*

Screens showing stabled horses as a principal subject with various attendants, warriors, and priests in a secondary role are known from the mid-Muromachi period on. This particular pair, cut down at the top, is thought to be as early as any, probably dating from the late fifteenth to early sixteenth century. The style of the figures in the screens is closely related to that seen in the earlier handscroll, "Fukutomi Zōshi" (cat. no 24), and it is certainly that of an artist trained in the Tosa school considerably earlier than the only datable screens of this type, the pair in the Hayashibara collection, Okayama, with inscriptions by priests living before 1638.

The horse was not only a divine steed—each major Shinto shrine had its sacred stable—but an important adjunct of military power. The narrative handscrolls of the Kamakura period showing military campaigns, such as the "Heiji Monogatari" in Boston, depict hundreds of horses used by the samurai warrior class. They were still a necessity in the Muromachi period, but the coming of muskets and cannons at the end of that time marked the end for the effective use of mounted warriors.

In these screens the close relationship of mounts to the aristocratic warrior class can be gauged by the activity of the foreground figures in court costume—some discussing the hunting falcons perched on their fists, others grooming the horses. On the other screen priests and nobles are playing *go* (the game of war) and a simpler chess-like game, *shōgi.* The controlled silhouettes of horses and figures are carefully placed in a decorative way that still retains something of the horizontal narrative style of the handscroll, all dominated by the rigid lines of porch, tatami, and stable. The format recalls a mid-Kamakura handscroll set, "Bai Sōshi" (Scroll of Horse Doctors), known from a segment in the Tokyo National Museum and fragments in private collections. This scroll of the "Bai Sōshi" depicts horses tethered in selected positions like those on the Cleveland screens.—SEL


Published:

Sherman E. Lee, *Japanese Decorative Style* (Cleveland, 1961), cat. no. 31.

Shimada Shūjirō, ed., *Zaigai Hihō,* vol. (Tokyo, 1969), pls. 24, 25.

Nakamura Tanio and Wakisaka Atsushi, *Sōjūga: Ryūko, Enkō,* Nihon Byōbu-e Shūsei, vol. 16 (Tokyo, 1977), colorpls. 63, 64, figs. 16, 17.

Takeda Tsuneo, ed., *Shōhei-ga,* Zaigai Nihon no Bijutsu, vol. 4 (Tokyo, 1980), colorpls. 114, 115.

Hamada Takashi, et al., *Zaigai Bijutsu Kaiga,* Genshoku Nihon no Bijutsu, vol. 27 (Tokyo, 1980), pls. 64, 65, 66.

Toda Teisuke, *Jimbutsuga: kara-ekei* Jimbutsu, Nihon Byōbu-e Shūsei, vol. 4 (Tokyo, 1980), pls. 91, 92.

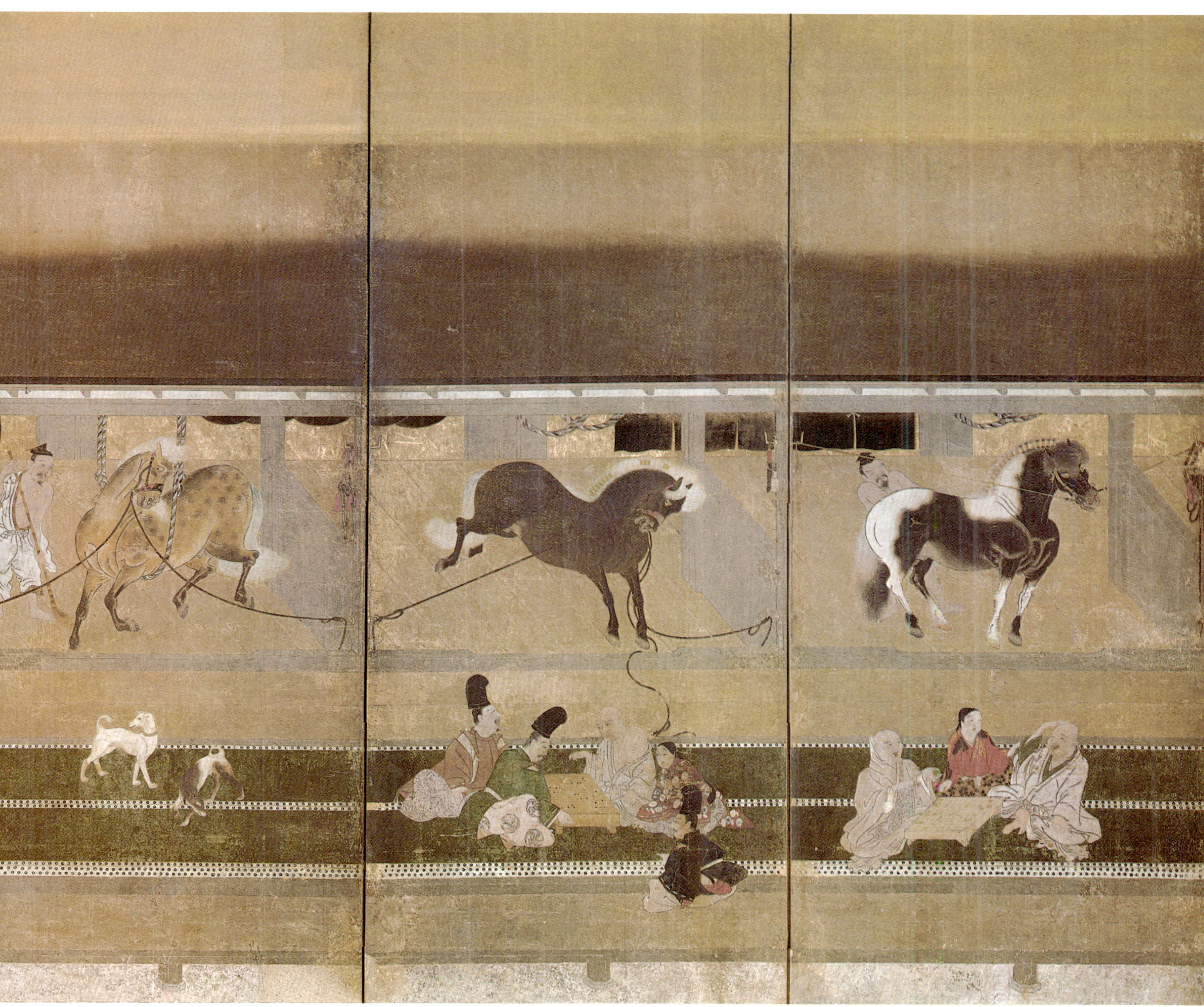

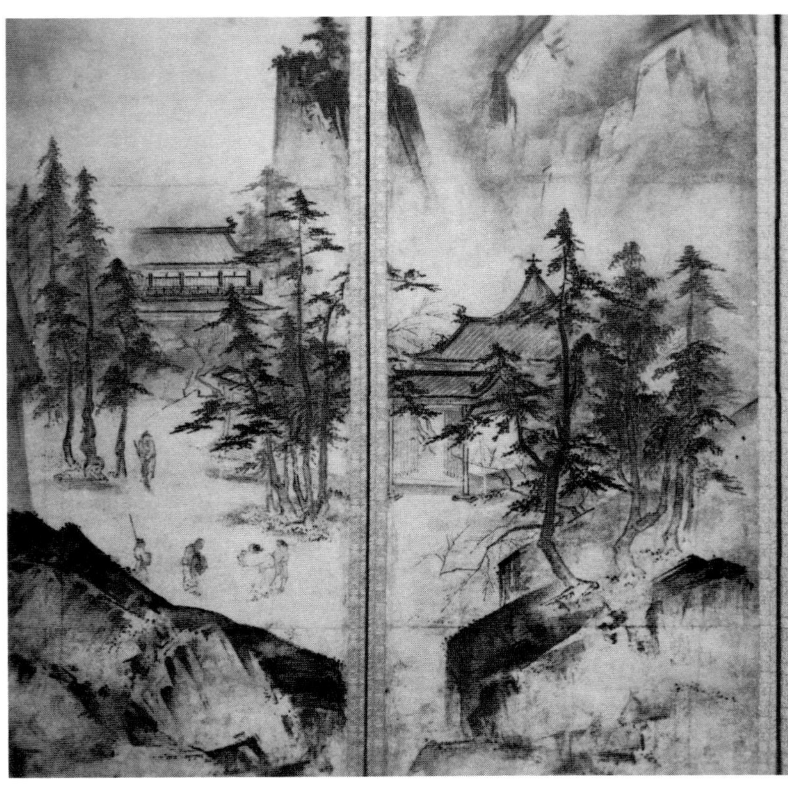

## 26
## Winter and Spring Landscape

*Shūbun (attributed to), fl. 1414-1463*
*Six-fold screen; ink and slight color on paper*
*H. 117.5 cm. W. 265.8 cm.*
*Ex collections: Shimazu, Tokyo; Osborne and Victor Hauge, Washington D.C.*
*Gift of the Norweb Foundation 58.476*

The fountainhead of the Muromachi monochrome school was the priest-painter Shūbun, Abbot of Shōkoku-ji in Kyoto. According to tradition he was the pupil of Jōsetsu (fl. ca. 1400) and teacher of the famous Sesshū (1420-1506). Shūbun's mastery as a painter is known only from three works, one a small painting made for Yoshimitsu, the third Ashikaga shogun, between 1394 and 1408. While some thirty works by Sesshū are recognized, only a handful of paintings attributable to Shūbun are known, and even these are not absolutely certain to be his though no one denies their quality or antiquity. This uncertainty is largely a result of our shadowy knowledge of the artist's life and of the seals used to sign the scrolls and screens attributed to him.

Shūbun traveled to Korea in 1423-1424. From 1430 to at least 1440, he was connected with the reconstruction of Shōkoku-ji, including the carving and painting of images. In 1430 he colored the image of the Zen patriarch Bodhidharma (Daruma) at Daruma-dera, Ōji. About 1440 he was in charge of producing a wooden image of Amida at Ungo-ji and was later asked to make two guardian kings. Shūbun was "painter-in-service" to the shogun as well as a leading artist for the monasteries. There are some contemporary references to his monochrome paintings of landscapes, birds and flowers, and bamboo in hanging scroll, screen, and wall-panel formats.

These sources, unanimous in their praise of Shūbun as a great master, emphasize the importance of his large-scale paintings. Until recently most modern critical attention was given to his small hanging scrolls, but this bias has been lately rectified. Screen paintings in his style are now recognized as the most fruitful objects of research as well as being the most developed and brilliant manifestations of the artist's work.

It was Shūbun who took a still amateurish Japanese monochrome Zen tradition of painting and transformed it into a large scale and thorougly accomplished style. For some of us, these landscape screens are the finest products of Japanese monochrome painting. This, combined with their rarity—only seven remotely acceptable examples are known—places them with the greatest Chinese scrolls of the Sung and Yüan dynasties on the pinnacle of Far Eastern landscape painting.

The two hanging scrolls, which are now the central panels of the Cleveland screen (panels three and four), were acquired in Japan by Osborne and Victor Hauge with the advice of Matsushita Takaaki, the late well-known scholar of Chinese and Japanese painting. Somewhat later, a pair of two-fold screens, obviously similar in style and content to the hanging scrolls, were acquired from the Shimazu collection by the same discerning collectors. Panel three obviously belonged to the two-fold screen now composing panels one and two. Panel four, also a winter scene, was not then recognized as contiguous to panel three; and none of the winter panels were seen as related to panels five and six as part of a single screen. A close examination of panel five revealed traces of pink color on the reaching branches of a leafless deciduous tree. This changed Summer to Spring, the time of the blossoming fruit tree, particularly of the favorite Chinese and Japanese motif, the prunus.

Since other pairs of screens by Shūbun were known to be paired seasonal subjects—Winter and Spring, Summer and

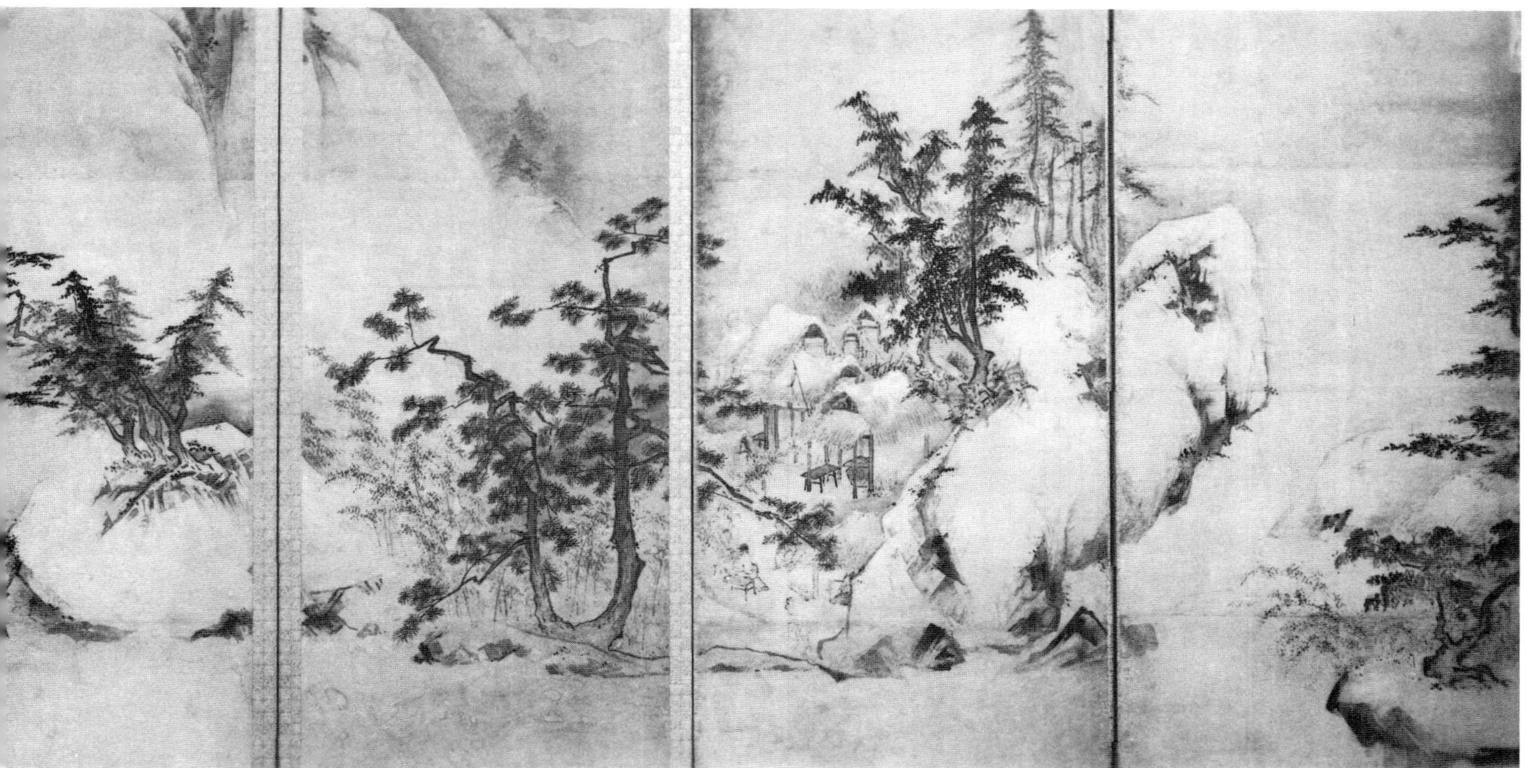

Autumn—a new study was made to relate the panels. Panel four was easily connected to three. By contiguous damages, the relationships of the high mountains, and the relevancy of the large rocks to the bridge leading to a path behind them, panel four was tentatively connected with five and six which were already together as the second two-fold screen from the Shimazu collection.

This connection is admittedly the most problematical one. Further, its uncertainty raises the possibility that panels five and six are from the second screen of the original pair. This suggestion made by Fred Martinson, Richard Stanley Baker, and Ronald Otsuka must be seriously considered. However, Baker's efforts to associate these paintings with Gakuō and the end of the fifteenth century are surely misguided.

The whole screen, despite some losses at the top and sides of the individual panels, was a breathtaking experience when first assembled. The frieze of re-united pine trees seemed to dance across the paper in an undulating movement, in and out, but always close to the spectator rather than distant as in the other screens in Japan—the closest in style being the three pairs from the Hara, Maeda, and Matsudaira collections.

The subject matter of the screen should be read from right to left as if it were a handscroll. Winter with its soft snow and cold mist grips the landscape of the first four panels, while the last two panels convey a softer message; a slight warmth in the ink tones changes the chilly steam of Winter to the soft breath of Spring.

Shūbun's style had a sound foundation. As painter to the shogun, he undoubtedly had access to the great collection of Chinese Southern Sung painting formed by Yoshimitsu. The brush style of Ma Yüan is evident in the "axe-hewn" strokes defining the rocks and Hsia Kuei's manner is to be seen in the trees. The general disposition of the trees against the nearby towering truncated mountains is remarkably similar to the two famous hanging scrolls by Li T'ang from Yoshimitsu's collection now kept at the Kōtō-in of Daitoku-ji in Kyoto. But the artist has not merely borrowed; he absorbs the essence of the Chinese masters and makes their technique and thoughts his own. To this base Shūbun added a breadth of scale in part inherent in the large scale decorative format of the folding screen. While grouped hanging scrolls with landscape subject matter were used by the Northern Sung masters, the folding screen was merely decorative in Chinese usage. It remained for the Japanese genius to make decoration and profundity rhyme. Shūbun was able to do this by avoiding the extremes of stylized composition and brushwork to which so many later Japanese monochrome painters were addicted. His ink varies from the lightest tones to the darkest; his brush can be soft or harsh at will. Complexity lies side by side with simplicity, fused by an almost magical ability to convince without display, an embodiment of intellect and emotion in perfect tension.—SEL


Published:

Nakamura Hideo, "The Landscape Screens Attributed to Shūbun," *Museum,* no. 14 (1952), p. 20.

Sherman E. Lee, "Winter and Spring by Shūbun," *The Bulletin of The Cleveland Museum of Art* 46, no. 8 (1952): 173-180.

____________, "Contrasts in Chinese and Japanese Art," *Journal of Aesthetics and Art Criticism* (Fall 1962): 4, fig. 2.

Shimada Shūjirō, ed., *Zaigai Hihō,* vol. 2 (Tokyo, 1969), 110, pls. 82, 83.

Ronald Y. Otsuka, "Winter and Spring: A Landscape Screen Attributed to Shūbun in The Cleveland Museum of Art," *Marasayas* 17 (1974-75): 85-92.

Shimizu Yoshiaki and Carolyn Wheelwright, eds., *Japanese Ink Paintings* (Princeton, 1976), cat. no. 12, pp. 108-117.

Shimada Shūjirō, *Suibokuga,* Zaigai Nihon no Shihō, vol. 3 (Tokyo, 1979), 126, colorpls. 27-28.

Hamada Takashi, et al., *Zaigai Bijutsu Kaiga,* Genshoku Nihon no Bijutsu, vol. 27 (Tokyo, 1980), pl. 47, detail, fig. 10.

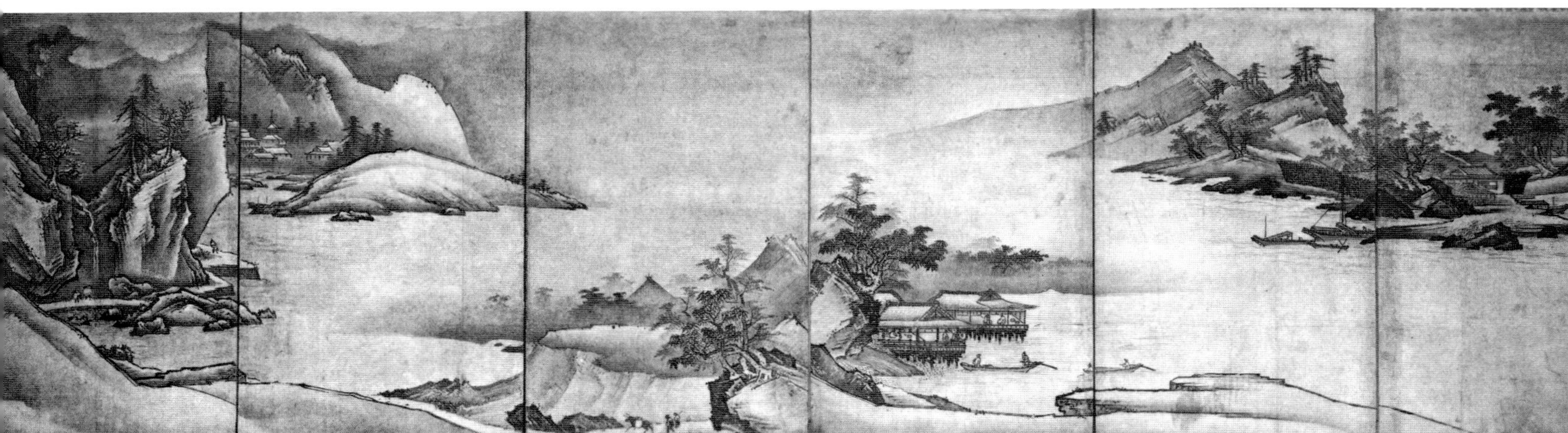

## 27
## Landscapes of the Four Seasons

*Ri Shūbun (Korean: Yi Su-mun), active mid-15th century*
*Pair of six-fold screens; ink and slight color on paper*
*H. 92.7 cm. W. 348.7 cm., each*
*Ex collection: Victor Hauge, Washington, D.C.*
*Purchase, John L. Severance Fund 76.92-.93*

The Korean painter Yi Su-mun is one of the few early Yi Dynasty (1392-1910) artists whose name and paintings have survived to any extent in Japan. An album of bamboo paintings now in the Tokyo National Museum bears an inscription dated 1424 stating that he was in Japan at that time, where he had become known as Ri Shūbun. This date is important both for its documentary value and because it suggests a relationship with the renowned fifteenth-century monk-painter Tenshō Shūbun, who participated in an official mission to Korea in 1423-1424 (see cat. no 26). Though both Shūbuns returned to Japan in 1424, it has not yet been determined whether they actually met one another.

All of Ri Shūbun's extant work is to be found in Japan except for these screens whose provenance was Japanese. Executed in a variety of formats (albums, hanging scroll, screens), they all share a number of compositional and stylistic features despite idiosyncracies of subject and brush manner.

The Cleveland screens of "Landscapes of Four Seasons" are assigned to Ri Shūbun's authorship on the basis of seals similar to the one found on the Tokyo National Museum's bamboo album. In addition they share fundamental resemblances with the other paintings; in the use of dramatically-shaped forms which are clearly separated or superimposed upon one another and frequently exaggerated in shape or positioning. Also tonal highlighting in patterned ink washes enhances object placement while creating a comprehensive ambience. The large, abridged mountains in the summer scene of the right-hand screen illustrate these features quite effectively. Ri Shūbun in these screens combines and transforms a knowledge of Chinese and Japanese painting modes through specific techniques and mannerisms of Japanese and Korean painting. Consequently they can be dated later in his career. Topographical and narrative vignettes in both screens remind us not only of the Southern Sung painter, Hsia Kuei (act. ca. 1180-1224) but also Shūbun, Geiami, Jasoku, Sesshū and other anonymous, later fifteenth-century painters. Basic transformations in painting were taking place at this time as Korean, Japanese, and Chinese paintings exerted their varying influences. The screens represent important expressions of that dynamic process.—MRC

Published:

Shimada Shūjirō, *Suibokuga,* Zaigai Nihon no Shihō, vol. 3 (Tokyo, 1979), nos. 27, 28.

Minamoto Toyomune, *Soga Jasoku*, Nihon Bijutsu Kaiga Zenshū, vol. 3 (Tokyo, 1980), nos. 6, 7, 8.

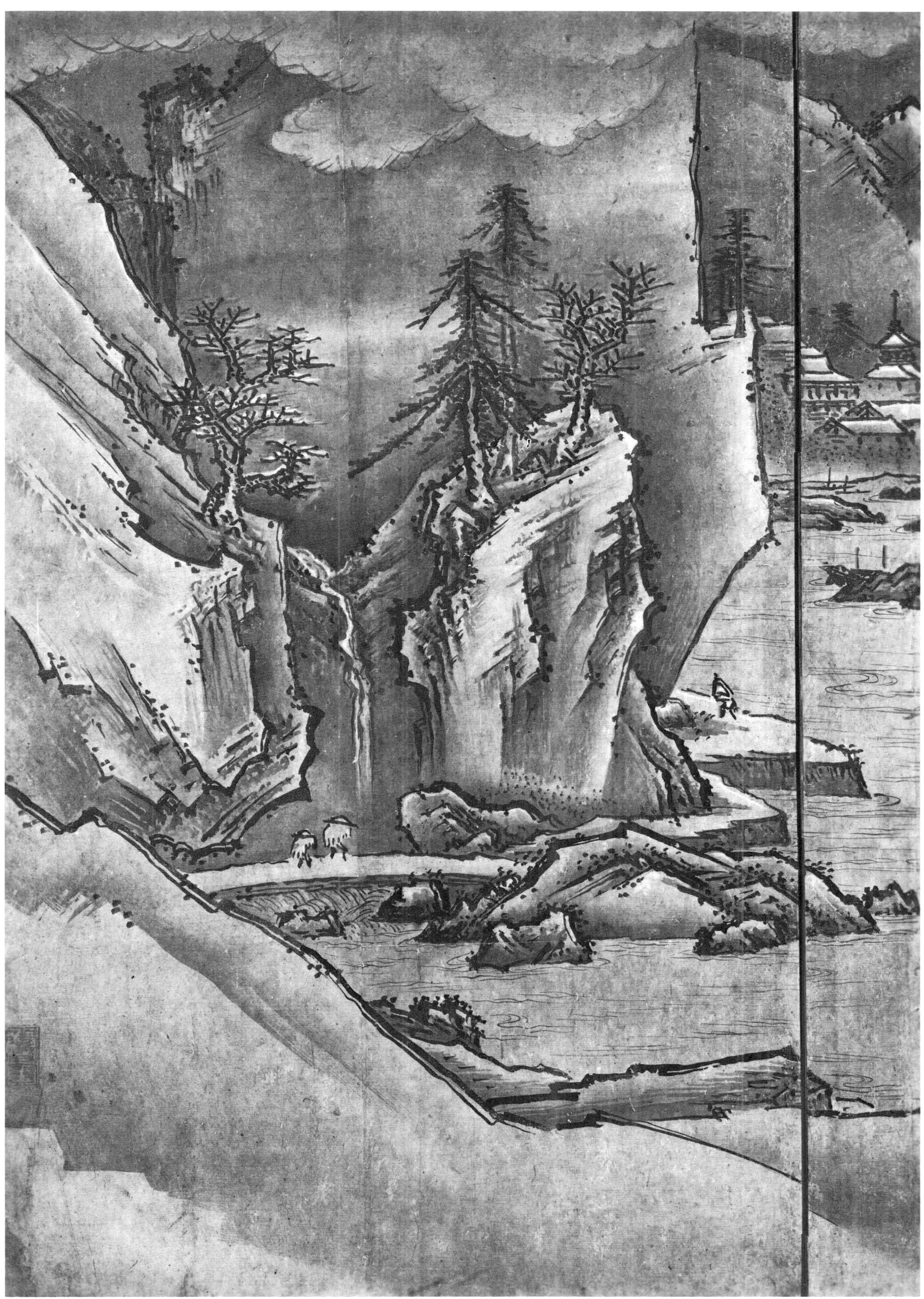

## 28

## Two Men Observing a Waterfall

*Sōami (Shinsō), 1485?-1525*
*Hanging scroll; ink and slight color on paper*
*H. 29 cm. W. 30.1 cm.*
*Ex collections: Hinohara; Sawada Chōkō*
*Purchase from the J. H. Wade Fund 77.30*

The theme of two Chinese gentlemen gazing at a distant waterfall is traditional in Far Eastern painting. Made popular by the Southern Sung academic painters Ma Yüan (fl. 1190-1225) and Hsia Kuei (ca. 1180-1224), such paintings typically depict a distinguished-looking man dressed in classical dress lost in thought as he watches a mountain waterfall. This figure has often been identified as Li Po (701-762), a major poet of the T'ang dynasty who wrote some verses about his experience seeing the famous waterfall at Mount Lu in Kiangsi province.

His poetry was known and revered by a small but influential group of Japanese educated in the Chinese classics. Some monks have even visited Mount Lu during their pilgrimage to China. As a consequence, the high regard maintained in Japan for Li Po seven hundred years after his death prompted collectors of imported Chinese paintings to appreciate compositions suggestive of the poet. Although these naturally exhibited a variety of compositional and stylistic features, common elements frequently included two male figures (one of which was a young attendant) placed in a lower quadrant of the painting near the viewer, a distant landscape of precipitous cliffs, encircling clouds, a waterfall, and remote peaks viewed across an expanse of water.

Here, following Hsia Kuei's painting style rather than that of Ma Yüan, Sōami depicts two Chinese men conversing while they look across an expanse of water towards the plummeting waterfall. Massive water-soaked clouds rise from the tumult, wafting off to enshroud forest groves and mountain bases at the edge of the river. A cluster of houses nestled among trees in front of the waterfall are partially visible through the mist, painted by Sōami in controlled, soft brushstrokes and ink washes. Other than the dark cliff and waterfall, the entire background of the painting displays a number of carefully registered ink tones acting as foils for the chute of water and the foreground narrative. This tendency of Sōami to eschew linear representation in order to achieve more naturalistic effects is a hallmark of his later work (cat. no. 29).

The boat moored among the rocks at the base of the ledge suggests that the men in the painting used it to come from the settlement across the water. The rather elaborate railing constructed around the perimeter of the ledge indicates that this spot was well-known for the view. Overhead an aged pine clings to a ledge wall, framing the observers. Below tufts of grasses and bamboo clusters are drawn over light ink washes, contrasting sharply with the abrupt shore bank and submerged rocks. These are firmly outlined, with somewhat exaggerated forms reminiscent of Ma-Hsia painting and Sōami's predecessor Geiami.

The general orientation of Sōami's paintings away from Ma Yüan-style painting can be seen in comparing this work with another painting of the identical subject dated before 1508. The composition and the clear, literal depiction of natural forms in that painting indicate a strong reliance on Ma Yüan and his followers in Japan among Shūbun-school artists. The more intimate nature of this small hanging scroll and its stylistic characteristics point to Sōami's conscious reworking of the Hsia Kuei tradition, particularly as he understood it through the work of Geiami and in his role as curator-connoisseur of the shogunal collection. Judging from his later involvement with predominantly ink-wash styles, this painting signals the beginnings of his mature work revealing a more poetic, *Yamato-e* temperament.—MRC


Published:

Tanaka Ichimatsu, Muromachi "Jigai ni Okeru Kanbaku-zu no Keifu," *Nihon Kaigashi Ronshu*, (Tokyo, 1966), fig. 138.

Matsushita Takaaki, *Suibokuga*, Nihon no Bijutsu, vol. 13 (Tokyo, 1967), pl. 129.

———, *Muromachi*, Nihon Kaigakan, vol. 5 (Tokyo, 1971), pl. 84.

Kanazawa Hiroshi, "Soami," *Nihon Bijutsu Kogei* 402 (1972): 34-46, pl. 5.

Matsushita Takaaki, *Josetsu, Shūbun, Sōami*, Suiboku Bijutsu Taikei, vol. 6 (Tokyo, 1974), pl. 123.

Shimada Shūjirō, *Suibokuga*, Zaigai Nihon no Shihō, vol. 3 (Tokyo, 1979), no. 66.

Hamada Takashi, et al, *Zaigai Bijutsu Kaiga*, Genshoku Nihon no Bijutsu, vol. 27 (Tokyo, 1980). fig. c 10.

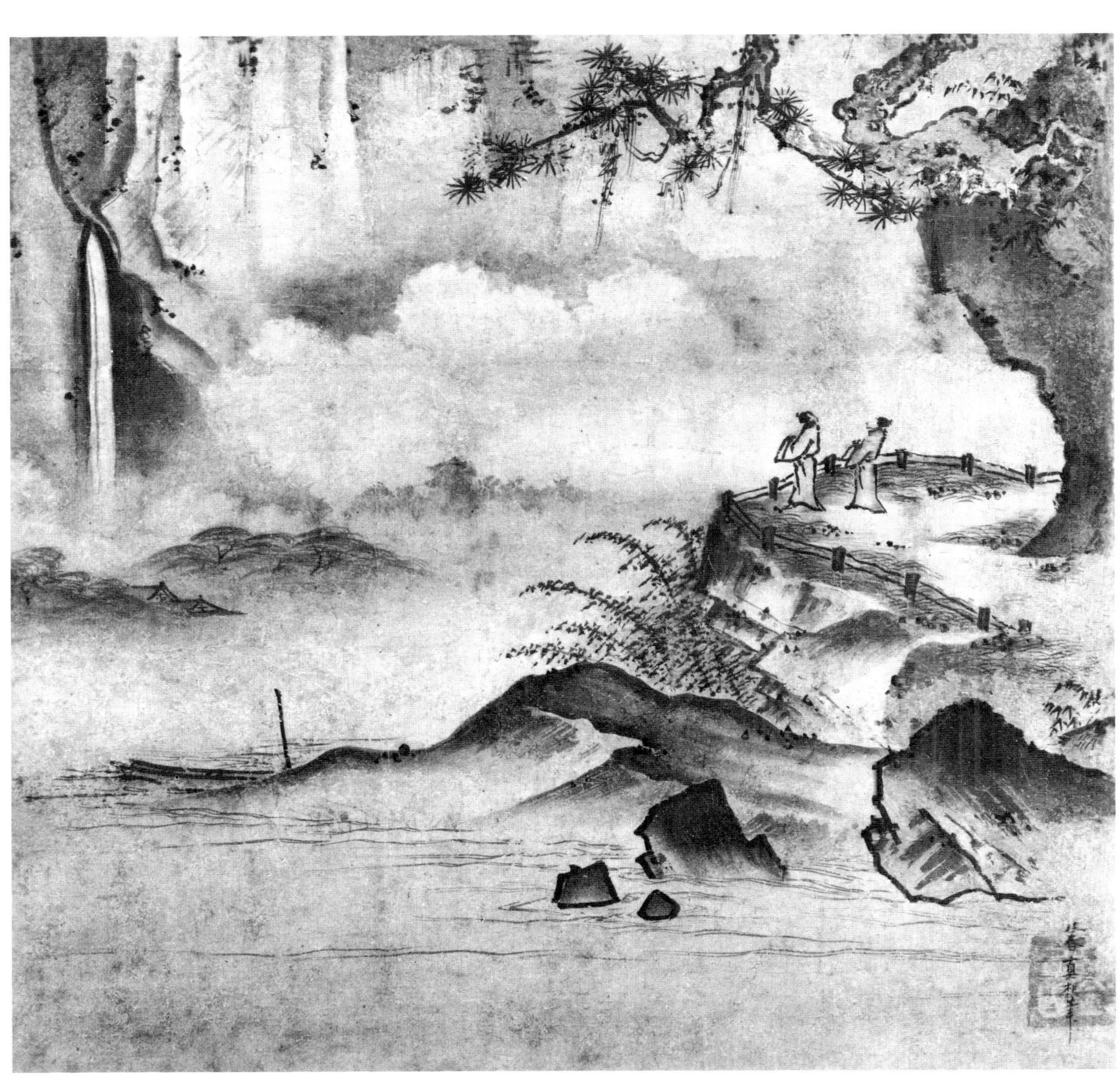

## 29
## Eight Views of the Hsiao and Hsiang Rivers

*Sōami (Shinsō), (1485?-1525)*
*Hanging scroll; ink on paper*
*H. 128.6 cm. W. 111.8 cm.*
*Ex collections: Viscount Matsudaira; Fukuoka Kōtei; Kosaku Junzō*
*Purchase, John L. Severance Fund 63.262*

In his capacity as curator-connoisseur of the shogunal collection, and as a painter in his own right, Sōami was frequently called upon to undertake important commissions. Some of these were modest in size (see cat. no. 28) while others represent projects more ambitious in scale. This large hanging scroll was originally a sliding wall partition in a temple room, one of several adjoining panels which together formed a coherent landscape theme. The painting represents Sōami's later, mature work which can be best seen in the superb panel set (now mounted as hanging scrolls) from the Daisen-in subtemple of the Daitoku-ji, Kyoto, completed about 1513.

In this scroll a summer landscape with groups of travelers crossing bridges and walking along lakeside paths is depicted. Fishermen work their nets at the foot of the mountains and in a distant inlet among the reeds and sandbars. The vegetation in the lowlands is lush, characterized by thick groves of trees, clusters of grasses, and abundant quantities of reeds interspersed among the river banks and projecting spits of land. Inland, low-lying hills give way through cloud banks to the rounded domes of the distant mountains, among which buildings are nestled. These allude to the "distant temple" theme of the popular *Eight Views of Hsiao and Hsiang,* (cat. no. 37 by Sesson) a painting subject introduced into Japan in the fourteenth century by imported Chinese scrolls depicting the confluence of these two rivers into Lake T'ung-ting in southern China.

Several famous Ch'an (Zen) monasteries were located in this area, making it a frequent destination for Japanese monks visiting China. The most renowned practitioner of the ink and brush style associated in Japan with Zen painting, the monk Mu-ch'i (act. late thirteenth century) lived in this area. His paintings were actively sought after by the Japanese, and indeed judging from stylistic elements evident in this scroll, Sōami knew his work first-hand in his capacity as keeper of the shogunal collection. He must also have been familiar with the ink-wash and dotting techniques of Kao Jan-hui, Kao K'o-kung and the Mi school painters, active in the late thirteenth and fourteenth centuries in southern China. The Mi school paintings feaure rounded, broadly-washed mountains whose bases are enveloped in clouds of mist, and whose flanks are covered with a profusion of horizontal ink dots. The artist's debt to Mu-ch'i can be detected in the long fibrous brushstrokes which define the contours and surfaces of the foreground banks and hills.

All of these stylistic features can be seen in this painting and, moreover, they comprise the constituent elements of the Daisen-in painting set, undoubtedly Sōami's major work. His transformation in this painting cycle of Chinese subject and brush technique into a thoroughly Japanese evocation of ambiance and place exerted a greater immediate influence on later sixteenth century Japanese painters than the work of his older contemporary Sesshū Tōyō (1420-1506). The late sixteenth century master Hasegawa Tōhaku (1539-1620) for instance records in his notebook, "Talks on Art," that Kanō Motonobu (cat. no. 38) was pointedly instructed to seek Sōami's advice in learning ink painting.

Whether this large scroll originally belonged to the Daisen-in set, as has been traditionally thought, will require further study. Although the painting surface has been extensively retouched and the borders cut down, it would be imprudent at this time to conclude that this scroll must then be attributed to a later follower of Sōami—especially since no reasonable candidate is known. It may be noted that there are Hsia Kuei painting elements seen in Sōami's earlier work (cat. no. 28) and evident here, and a strong reference to a seasonal (summer) theme rather than to a clear *Eight Views* scene. This peaceful view of man and nature points, as no other known work, towards Sōami's later, major achievements. The painting has an impressive history of authentication and provenance.

—MRC

Published:
*Kokka* 6, no. 64 (January, 1895): 293, pl. 1.
Iitsuka Beiu, ed., *Nihonga Taisei,* vol. 3 (Tokyo, 1931), pt. 1, pl. 60.
Shimada Shūjirō, ed., *Zaigai Hihō,* vol. 2 (Tokyo, 1969), pt. 1, p. 122, pt. 2, pl. 94.
Sherman E. Lee, "Zen in Art: Art in Zen," *The Bulletin of The Cleveland Museum of Art* 59, no. 9 (1972): 255-56, figs. 16, 16a.
Shimizu Yoshiaki and Carolyn Wheelwright, eds., *Japanese Ink Paintings* (Princeton, 1976), cat. no. 27.
Shimada, Shūjirō, *Suibokuga,* Zaigai Nihon no Shihō, vol. 3 (Tokyo, 1979), colorpl. 66.

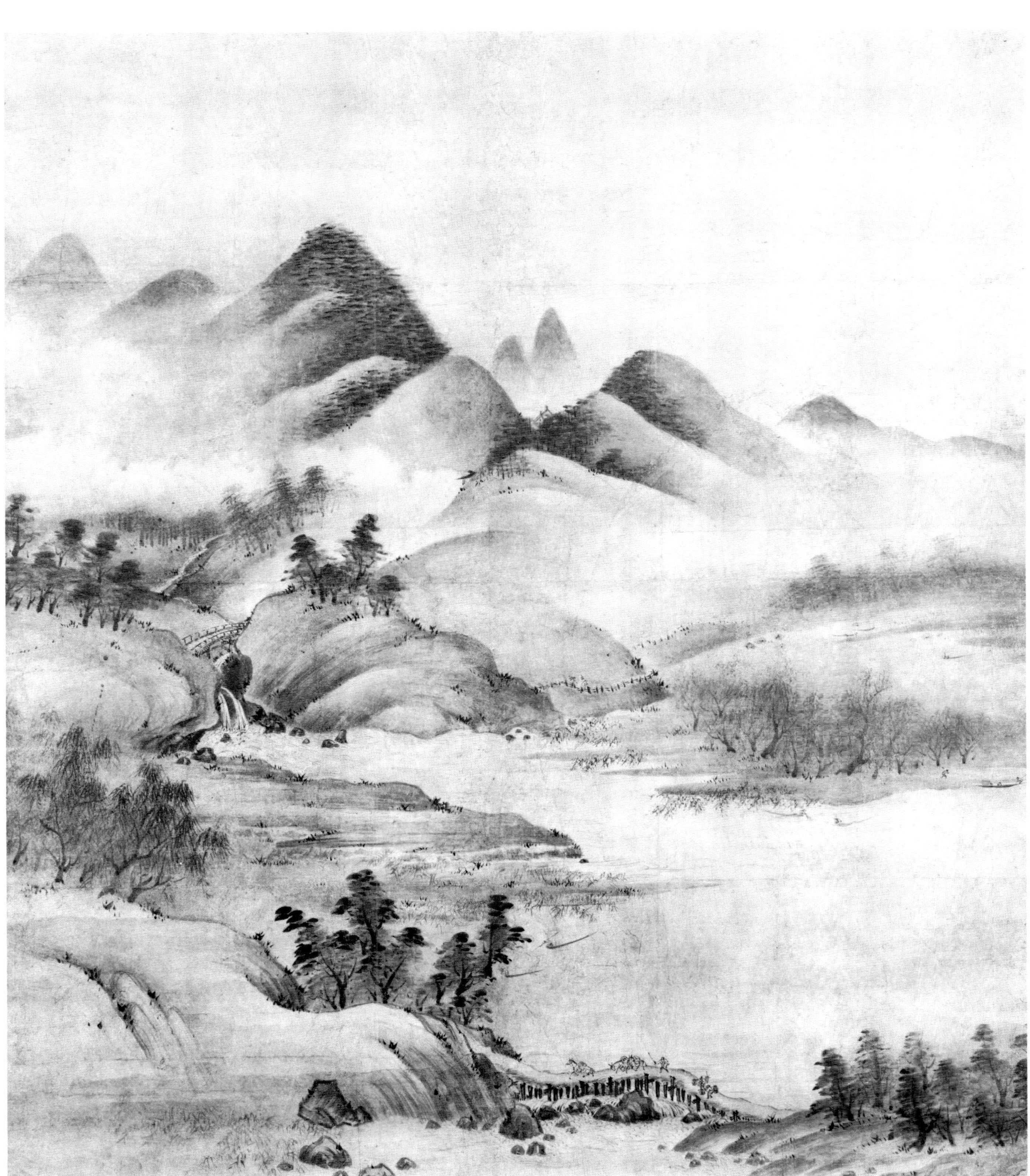

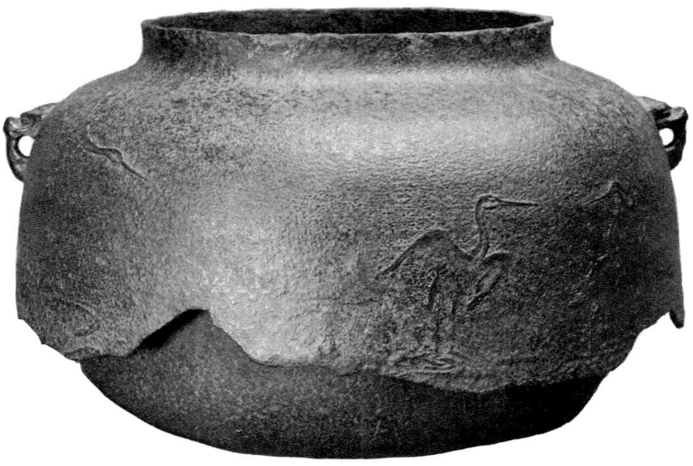

30

## Iron Kettle: Ashiya type

*Muromachi Period, 1392-1573*
*Iron*
*H. 18 cm. Diam. 30.2 cm.*
*Purchase from the J. H. Wade Fund 80.11*

Special types of iron kettles for the heating of water during the tea ceremony were produced as early as the fourteenth century and were based at first on Chinese and Korean prototypes. The principal center of ancient production was Ashiya in old Chikuzen province (modern Fukuoka, Kyūshū) where sturdy vessels with relief decoration were made in sand and clay molds used only once. Like Chinese bronzes, each iron kettle is unique. The early vessels are prized because of reverence for age, as well as for their subtle decoration, low, weighty profiles, and pleasingly rough surface textures. In addition to these characteristics, at least two major indices of early dates are recognized: the demon (or "monkey") mask handles should be simple and powerful; the mouth of the vessel very wide in proportion to the total diameter. This particular tea kettle qualifies on all counts and in addition has a particularly striking but understated design of flying and standing cranes in water and on land-spits. They seem to emerge from the rough iron surface as though growing from within and are cunningly placed in a markedly asymmetrical arrangement. The "skirt," attractively damaged, remains in contrast to some other examples where it has been completely broken off and ground down. The interior reveals heavy lime deposits from the repeated boiling of water with a high calcine and mineral content.

Perhaps no other object in this exhibition reveals so completely those remarkable aesthetic qualities prized by the devotees of tea. Rough but refined, strong but subtle; natural but cunningly manufactured—this is a particularly rare object in the West. While it is regrettable that this kettle has passed out of use to become an object encased in a vitrine, it now serves another useful purpose as a test of understanding the tea ceremony aesthetic in Japanese art.—SEL

Published:
Hosomi Ryōichi, *Cha no Yugama* (Tokyo, 1974), pl. 11.

31

## Storage Jar: Shigaraki ware

*Muromachi Period, 14th-15th centuries*
*Stoneware*
*H. 42 cm. Diam. 39 cm.*
*Purchase, John L. Severance Fund 73.18*

Medieval Japanese ceramics have traditionally been identified and divided among "Six Old Kilns," one of which is Shigaraki. Shigaraki is, in turn, a convenient term for identifying a fertile mountain valley east of Kyoto in Shiga perfecture, laden with feldspathic clay, and populated by farmers and foresters as far back as the eighth century.

Shigaraki enjoyed convenient proximity to Uji, a major tea cultivation region south of Kyoto along the Uji river. By the fourteenth century the consumption of tea reached new heights as it became an increasingly commercial item in Japan due to its expanded social appeal. The demand for ceramic vessels suitable for transport and proper storage of tea leaves increased. Political tribute and indeed taxes were also commonly paid for with tea leaves. As a result Shigaraki emerged by the late fifteenth century as a growing center of ceramic production, linked specifically to the tea industry.

Excavations done over the last two decades indicate that ceramic production in the fourteenth and fifteenth centuries focused on kitchen wares, jars associated with religious use, and grain storage jars such as this Cleveland example. Kiln sites were located throughout the valley and naturally depended on the presence of satisfactory clay and quantities of wood. The Shigaraki farmers undoubtedly comprised the valley's potters, but household and village-based workshops soon followed. Although technical information arrived from the advanced ceramic production centers at Seto and Tokoname, Shigaraki artisans can only be termed semi-professional up until the late fifteenth century.

This large storage vessel *(tsubo)* is a product of just such an anonymous farmer-artisian who in all likelihood learned from potters in the Tokoname kiln area the coiling technique used to build this generous form. The vessel is comprised of four successive sections of clay coils joined to one another. Each section was scraped smooth inside and out with a wood or bamboo paddle, and then allowed to dry slightly before the

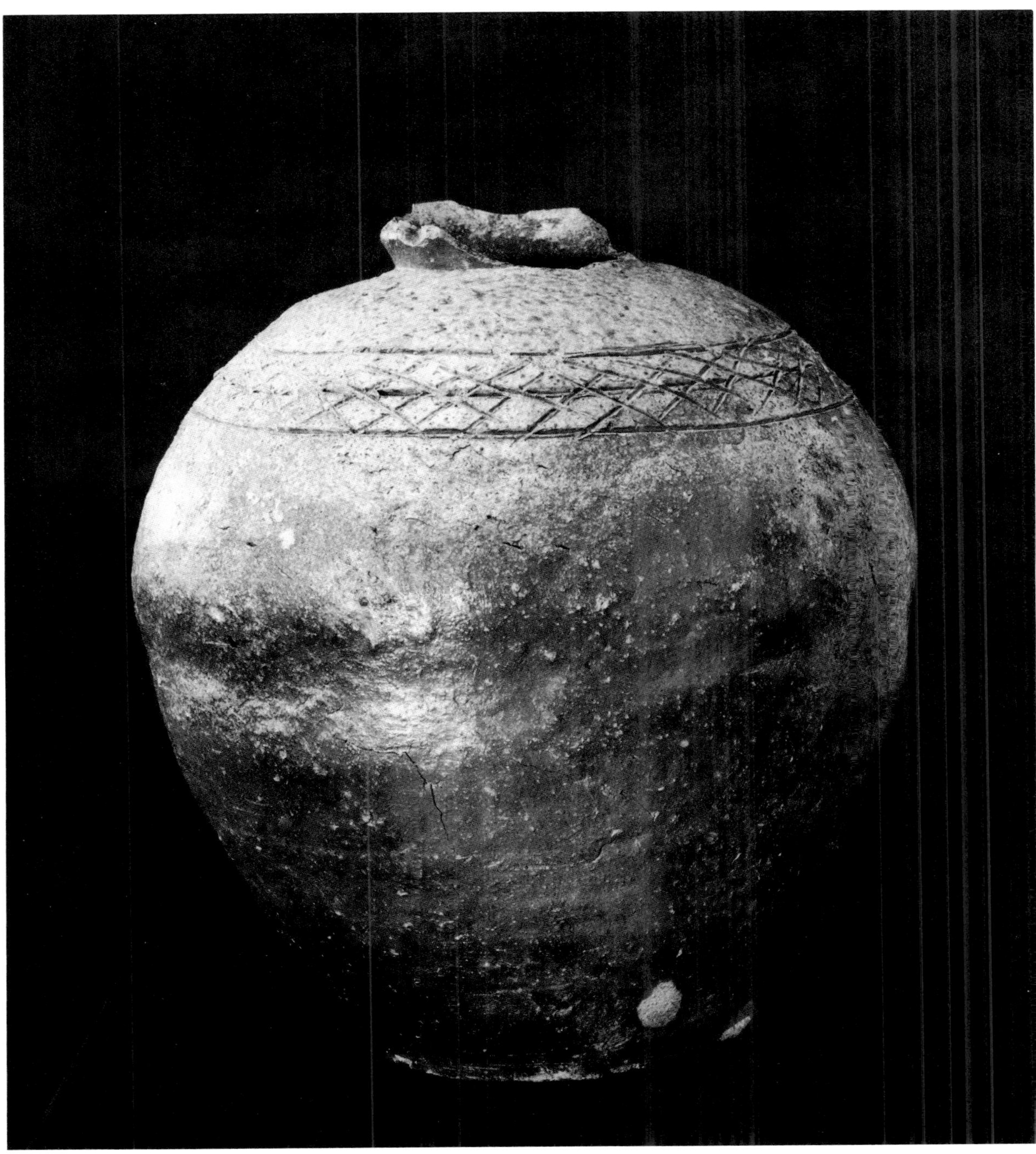

next series of coils was added. The smaller clay coils forming the neck were added last. The base supporting the entire structure is a simple clay disk. The appealing, sturdy appearance of Kamakura and Muromachi period Shigaraki storage jars is due in large part to this coiling technique.

Another aspect of "Six Old Kilns" wares which attracts admirers is the warm surface characteristics of Shigaraki clay. These include the white melted granules of feldspar scattered throughout the clay body, surface eruptions, linear splits, and the deep natural color markings on a reddish-brown skin. These are all visible on this storage jar in addition to a matte surface above the shoulder of the pot where wood ash present in the kiln atmosphere has adhered to the molten clay surface during firing, sometimes forming beads of natural "glassy" green glaze. The double "rope" design incised at shoulder level is rather unusual for a vessel of this size and purpose. A meaning for the rope design beyond a purely decorative one has yet to be substantiated. This vessel was used originally for seed or grain storage, antedating the high tea fashions of the sixteenth century in Kyoto, Nara, and Osaka. Judging from its size, shape, color, and clay it may be assigned a mid-fifteenth century provenance from the southern kilns of the Shigaraki valley where vessels and shards possessing similar characteristics have been excavated. The Minami-Matsuo kiln in Nagano district, active beginning in the fourteenth century, may well be the specific production site.—MRC


Published:

Kyoto National Museum, *Special Exhibition: Earthenware of Ancient Japan* (Kyoto, 1963), fig. 171.

Daniel Rhodes, *Tamba Pottery: The Timeless Art of a Japanese Village* (Tokyo, 1970), p. 10.

Sherman E. Lee, "Some Japanese Tea Taste Ceramics," *The Bulletin of The Cleveland Museum of Art* 60, no. 9 (1973): 269, fig. 1.

Victor and Takako Hauge, *Folk Traditions in Japanese Art* (New York, 1978), cat. no. 56.

## 32
## Nō Mask: Okina

*Muromachi Period, 1392-1573*
*Wood (*Celtis *or hackberry) with hemp beard*
*H. 20.3 cm.*
*Purchase from the J. H. Wade Fund 77.33*

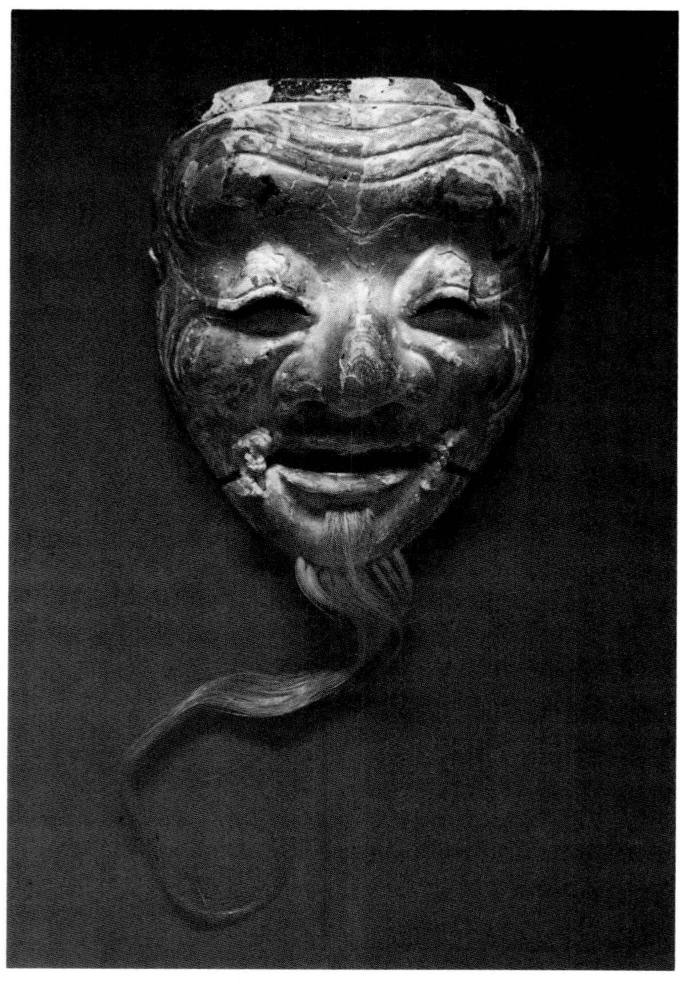

The three masks in this and the following two entries represent the sculptor's art at the service of one of the most remarkable of dramatic inventions—the Nō play. Some background, however slight, is essential to begin understanding these subtle sculptures. A flat description conveys little of the wonder and power of Nō. A small stage separates the drama from an audience seated on the floor, or on grassy ground. The roofed stage has a solitary backdrop representing the sacred pine tree of Kasuga Shrine at Nara. A corridor runway connects to the stage on the spectators' left. All performers move over the runway to the stage: assistants, and subsidiary actors, including the *waki*, the foil for the principal actor, the *shite*. When all save the principal actor have appeared, the music—measured, high-pitched, rich with intervals—begins; then the principal actor appears moving immeasurably slowly along the runway. Masked, gorgeously gowned, the principal intones the assigned lines of the play to the music of the orchestra and chorus. The Nō texts are short, the plots are simple; but the plays may last as long as two hours—and the minimum program is two plays with a comic interlude called *Kyōgen*. The fascination of Nō for the Western avant-garde has been attested to, from Ezra Pound to Karl-Heinz Stockhausen. Its appeal lies in its being so traditional, so conservative, so ritualized, that it paradoxically becomes an avant-garde image of timelessness, of ultimate knowing.

Nō drama shares, with the tea ceremony and the monochrome ink landscapes of the Muromachi period, the conscious coalition of mysticism and aestheticism associated with Zen Buddhism. While many of the earliest Nō masks are owned by Shinto shrines, attesting to its folkish and animistic origins in *Sarugaku* and *Dengaku*, Nō stands or falls as another aspect of Zen. The careful ritual of the tea ceremony and the slow, measured, and predetermined movements of Nō are counterparts to the rigid discipline of a Zen regimen whose end is sudden intuitive enlightenment. Nō retained its native Shinto origins, its feudal and aristocratic poetic texts, and so continued in vigor and creativity through the periods succeeding Muromachi: the Momoyama (1573-1615), Edo (1615-1868), and modern. Its literary roots in the old tales of demons, ghosts, warriors, clan history, purification, and feudal loyalty were both Shinto and Buddhist, folk and aristocratic.

The most important single object of art used in Nō is the mask. Small in size and light in weight, the Nō mask exists in at least 125 subjects divisible into four main categories: old persons, women, warriors, and demons. Most of the earlier masks are found in temples, and particularly shrines, for their Shinto connections are dominant, and they served the same interlude functions at sacred Shinto ceremonies as *Gigaku* did for Buddhist ones. But the adoption of Nō by the shogun's court in the particular person of Zeami (1363-1443, an historical founder of Nō drama) and his tradition sealed the intimate relationship of Nō to Zen.

The earlier masks are more varied and individual in their expressions and are derived from the numerous sculptural traditions available to the carvers of the early Muromachi period in the fifteenth century. The dating and attribution of Nō masks is still heavily overlaid with family traditions and scholarly myths. While it seems fruitless in our present state of knowledge to try to establish any sure priorities, certain technical and stylistic origins seem indicated.

Technically, the carving of masks was intimately related to the carving of Buddhist and Shinto sculpture. In the later Heian period the "pieced-wood technique" of making images took precedence over the single-block method and far more flexibility became possible. There was also a possibility of greater subtlety and virtuosity in the suggestion of light and shade by the carving. The latter is particularly significant for the successful production of the Nō mask, for its limited changing qualities over a two-hour performance period are confined to the manner in which it reflects or cradles the light it receives in its various positions depending on the movement of the actors' heads. The use of subtle polychromy is also a technical inheritance from the making of images. We can be reminded forcefully of this by the fact that some great painters, notably Shūbun (see cat. no. 26), were also painters of images.

In 1374 Ashikaga Yoshimitsu, the first shogun of the Muromachi period, commanded the appearance of Kan'ami (died ca. 1384) as the old man in "Okina" at the Imakumano Shrine at Kyoto. "Okina" is still the one indispensable Nō drama. The "Okina" mask portrays a humorous, superhuman Old Man, a combination of the wisdom of old age with the humor of the village wit. Usually he appears before the main plays as the one who invokes divine blessings on the performance and by extension, the world as stage. The form of the mask is particularly traditional and retains the movable chin characteristic of many of the earlier *Bugaku* masks going back to the Nara period. This particular one has been traditionally dated to early Muromachi and its technical features—even polychromy, deeply carved reverse, and relatively naturalistic appearance—suggest an attribution to a period before 1450.—SEL

Published:
Shirasu Masako, *Nō-men* (Tokyo, 1963), colorpl. 1.

33
## Nō Mask: Waka-onna

*Muromachi Period, 1392-1573*
*Wood (paulownia) with polychromy*
*H. 19.8 cm.*
*Purchase, John L. Severance Fund 72.69*

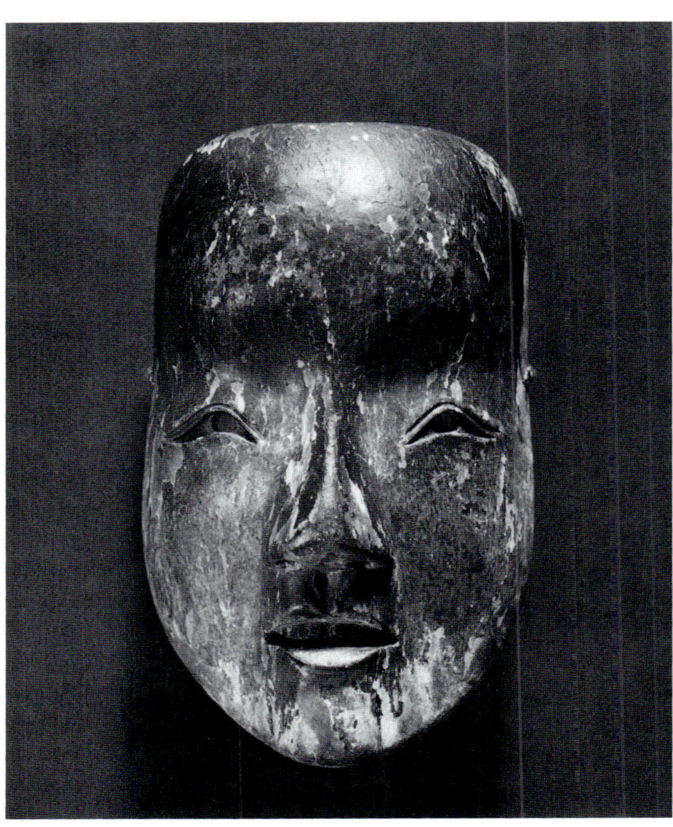

This female mask, a *waka-onna*, is one of the varieties of Nō masks of a young woman, not a maiden. Perzynski's description of the type is applicable: (Frederick Perzynski, *Japanische Masken*, Berlin and Leipzig, 1925, II, 198)

> The charming face of a very young woman with the soft features of a girl. The arching forehead with artificial brow appears extremely high because of the intentionally emphasized narrowness of the oval face. The wide-spaced eyes lie on an almost straight line. The lips are only very slightly parted and, seen at a distance, the mouth appears closed. The corners of the mouth end usually in sharp points. The lower lip protrudes somewhat. The complexion is a mellow yellow-white, the upper teeth are darkened.

The description is of the classic *waka-onna*, and the early date assigned to this mask, first half of the fifteenth century, is accounted for by variations that would have been considered heterodox by later carvers, but which it shares with the *waka-onna* masks of the same date preserved in such temples or shrines as those of Rinnō-ji (Nikkō, Tochigi prefecture) and Suwasugi Shrine (Fukui prefecture). The former in particular has a firm *terminus ad quem* of 1469, the date of its presentation to the temple. Common to all *waka-onna* masks and particularly to the Cleveland example, are the crinkly, slightly humorous effect around the eyes, and the almost-smiling mouth it shares in common with the Rinnō-ji mask. Fortunately the Cleveland *waka-onna*, like the two previously mentioned in Japan, has not been repainted; the unearthly subtlety of her partially enigmatic expression can be enjoyed without the more explicit directions of later hands.

The *waka-onna* mask is used principally in "woman plays", notably "Matsukaze," "Futari Shizuka," "Hagoromo," "Kakitsubata," "Izutsu," and others. "Hagoromo" is particularly famous and tells the story of a fisherman who finds a robe of feathers hanging upon a pine tree at the beach of Miho. He announces his intention of keeping it, but a beautiful woman appears and begs him to give back the robe, saying that without it she cannot return to heaven. The fisherman, moved by her grief, agrees to give her the robe if she will dance for him. She performs several dances before she disappears into the heavens. Some of the last lines read:

> Over the mountain of Ashitaka,
> Over the high peak of Fuji,
> Her form grows indistinct.
> She mingles with the mists of heaven,
> She is lost to sight.

(Donald Keene, *Nō: The Classical Theatre of Japan*, Tokyo, 1966, p. 121)—SEL

Published:
Donald Jenkins, *Masterworks in Wood: China and Japan* (Portland, Oreg., 1976), cat. no. 56.

34

## Nō Mask: Ko-beshimi

*Muromachi Period, 1392-1573*
*Wood with polychromy*
*H. 20.4 cm.*
*Purchase, John L. Severance Fund 72.70*

This mask takes us to a totally different realm of Nō, (see cat. no. 33) to that of the demon—in this case, Ko-beshimi (smaller demon, as contrasted with Ō-beshimi, a larger demon mask). Perzynski's description covers most of its attributes: (Frederick Perzynski, *Japanische Masken,* Berlin and Leipzig, 1925, II, 88-89.)

> This demon mask, somewhat softer in expression [than that of Ō-beshimi], is that of a considerably humanized devil with smooth forehead, two horizontal, sickle-shaped frontal furrows continuing the brows above the wrinkle on the bridge of the nose, usually with somewhat smaller metal eyes than those of the Ō-beshimi, looking straight ahead, and with a broad but not overhanging nose with large but no longer bestially vibrating nostrils as those of the Ō-beshimi. The mouth is still tightly pinched, the chin thrust forward as a smooth, ample plane. From the sides of the nose to the bitterly down-turned corners of the mouth run two deep wrinkles, curving almost half-way into the chin. A few long folds furrow the fleshy cheek, and frame but no longer thrust it forward and up to ear and eye as an island.
>
> Brows outspread and a sharply delineated mustache and chin beard are all painted with a brush. In keeping with the smooth surface treatment of the mask, the ears are often very summarily modelled, without any indication of the auditory canal. The complexion runs from light to chocolate to red-brown to red. The folds are enhanced with red or generally darker tones. The Ko-beshimi mask also calls for a red wig.

Perzynski then goes on to mention the probable relationship of the *beshimi* type to that of Daruma (Bodhidharma), the legendary Indian founder of the Zen sect, often represented in Japanese art (especially painting) as glaring without eyelids—a reference to his cutting them off after sleepily failing in his meditation on the Buddha. This suggestion is, in my judgment, later Zen interpolation. For not only are sculptural, and to a certain extent painted, representations of Daruma not common before the middle of the fifteenth century, but a clear and easier relationship exists between the *beshimi* type and that of the head of the Buddhist guardian image. Further, the *Ko-beshimi* mask seems to have been used rather early, an innovation by Zeami himself.

The dating of this well-known *Ko-beshimi* mask seems reasonably early in view of its clear and close derivation from thirteenth-century guardian images. It is especially important to recognize the relative freedom and lack of smoothness in the Cleveland mask—again speaking of its relationship to earlier and still unformed formulae within the emerging Nō discipline. Still, it seems somewhat later than the *waka-onna* and should be placed in the second half of the fifteenth century, well before the somewhat wax-work types one encounters in the masks of the Edo period. Its nearest counterpart is the *beshimi* mask belonging to Narazuhiko Shrine in Nara prefecture.

The *Ko-beshimi* mask was used in various demon dramas, especially "Kuzu," "Ukai," and in the classic spider-demon drama, "Tsuchigumo." Keene's summary can reveal but little of the terror produced by stage-craft in this play (Donald Keene, *Nō: The Classical Theatre of Japan,* Tokyo, 1966, p. 269).

> The warrior Raikō is afflicted by a mysterious illness. A priest (principal actor) comes and tells Raikō that his illness is caused by a great spider (Tsuchigumo). Raikō sees through the priest's disguise and recognizes that he is the spider. They fight and the wounded spider flees. In the second part a retainer of Raikō tracks the spider to his lair and kills it.—SEL

Published:
Shirasu Masako, *Nō-men* (Masks for Nō Plays), (Tokyo, 1963), pl. 33.
Donald Jenkins, *Masterworks in Wood: China and Japan* (Portland, Oreg., 1976), cat. no. 57.

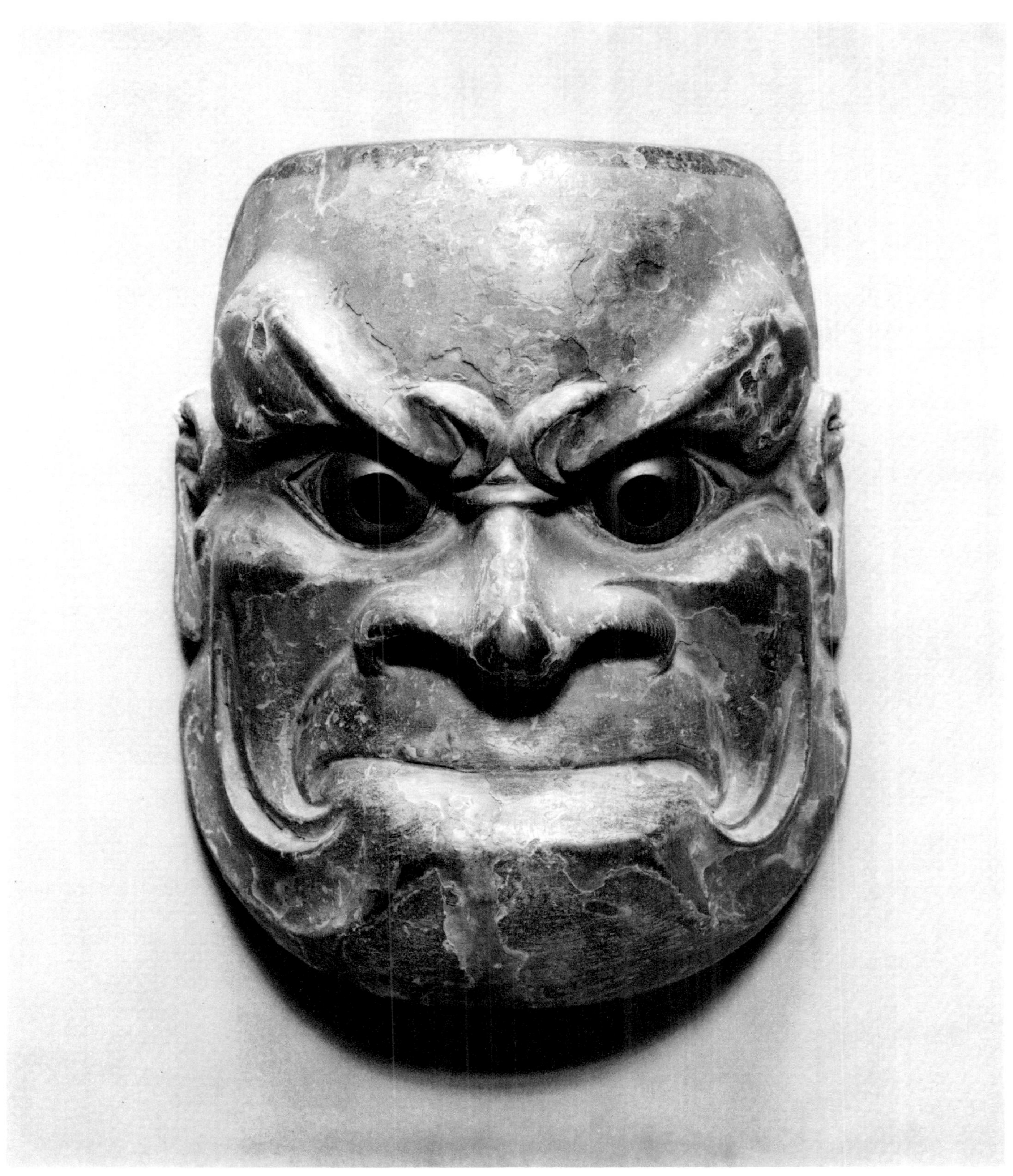

35

## Haboku Landscape

*Shūgetsu, died ca. 1510*
*Hanging scroll; ink on paper*
*H. 59.6 cm. W. 26.8 cm.*
*Ex collecton: Tanaka Gōhei*
*Purchase from the J. H. Wade Fund 76.59*

The artist Shūgetsu Tōkan is said to have been a samurai from Kyūshū who became a direct pupil of Sesshū Tōyō, Japan's most renowned ink painter. Like Sesshū he is reported to have gone to China, but it is not certain when this occurred or for how long he remained there. The important "West Lake" painting in the Ishikawa Prefectural Museum has traditionally been assigned to Shūgetsu on stylistic grounds, although it bears no signature or seal of the artist. However an inscription on the painting states that it was done in Peking in 1496, thus establishing that the artist of the painting was active in the last decade of the fifteenth century.

Other extant paintings attributed to Shūgetsu unfortunately contain no further historical information, especially as it may relate to other works or his early training with Sesshū. Both men executed landscapes in various styles, Buddhist and Taoist figures, and bird and flower subjects. It is recorded that Shūgetsu was skillful at rendering dragons and tigers and, significantly, the "flung ink" *(haboku)* painting technique. This painting manner became well-known in Japan following the importation from China of the *Eight Views of Hsiao Hsiang* handscrolls by Mu-ch'i and Yü-chien, thirteenth century monk-painters. Yü-chien's paintings in this difficult brush manner were avidly sought after by collectors, and copied by Japanese ink painters. They feature the dispersion of ink washes of varying tonal intensity and wetness across a blank painting surface, defining in quick, rudimentary fashion a landscape. The successful layering of the washes coupled with abrupt linear accents posed formidable challenges for Japan's amateur ink painters.

Surely the Japanese painting most famous for mastering this Chinese technique and transforming it into a purely Japanese statement is Sesshū's 1495 "Haboku Landscape" in the Tokyo National Museum collection. This Cleveland scroll follows that landmark piece closely in subject, description, and composition. Both illustrate river scenes with sandbars and ledges, at the base of which two rooftops can be seen. A pole with a small flag displayed on it identifies this as a tavern where travelers may stop to refresh themselves. Behind the huts a rock outcropping laden with trees and vegetation looms over the scene.

While this painting should properly be seen as an homage to Sesshū's painting, it achieves a character all its own through its use of a more isolated image and remarkable suffusions of ink washes into the soft paper. These are thoughtfully organized and registered in controlled tonal intensities, balanced by spared-out areas and by the dark flat rocks in the foreground. When compared with Sesshū's architectonic painting these arrangements of ink assume less narrative meaning in favor of expressing more personal sentiments. The placement and calligraphic style of Shūgetsu's signature echo this intention.

If we are to believe the historians, Shūgetsu's *haboku* landscapes were so accomplished they were often mistaken for Sesshū's. These records also state that Sesshū's successors at his studio in western Japan became proficient at the *haboku* technique by studying Shūgetsu's paintings rather than the master's. Judging from extant sixteenth century *haboku* paintings by Sesshū-school followers and artists such as Unkoku Tōgan (1547-1618), this is certainly reasonable. Indeed Sesshū's work, including the 1495 painting, quickly became personal documents or coveted collectors' items in the sixteenth century, whereas those paintings done by his students frequently proved to be more available and influential in conveying his legacy to later generations of artists and admirers.—MRC

Published:
Tanaka Ichimatsu and Nakamura Tanio, *Sesshū-Sesson,* Suiboku Bijutsu Taikei, vol. 7 (Tokyo 1973), fig. 67.
Matsushita Takaaki, *Muromachi Suibokuga* (Tokyo, 1960), pl. 44.
Yomiura Press, *Sekai no Gasei Sesshū-ten,* (Osaka, 1971) cat. no. 23.
Hamada Takashi, et al., *Zaigai Bijutsu Kaiga,* Genshoku Nihon no Bijutsu, vol. 27 (Tokyo, 1980), fig. c14.

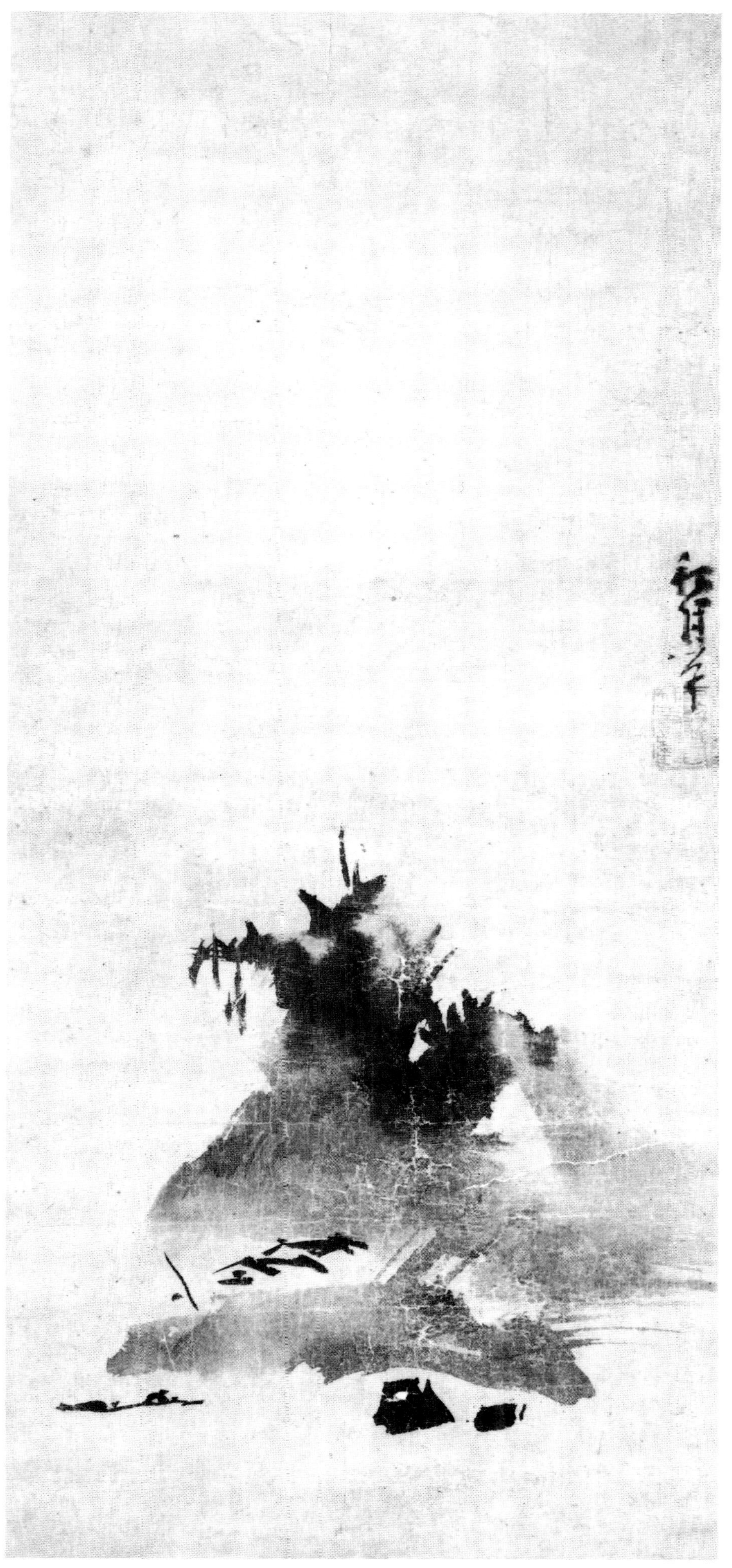

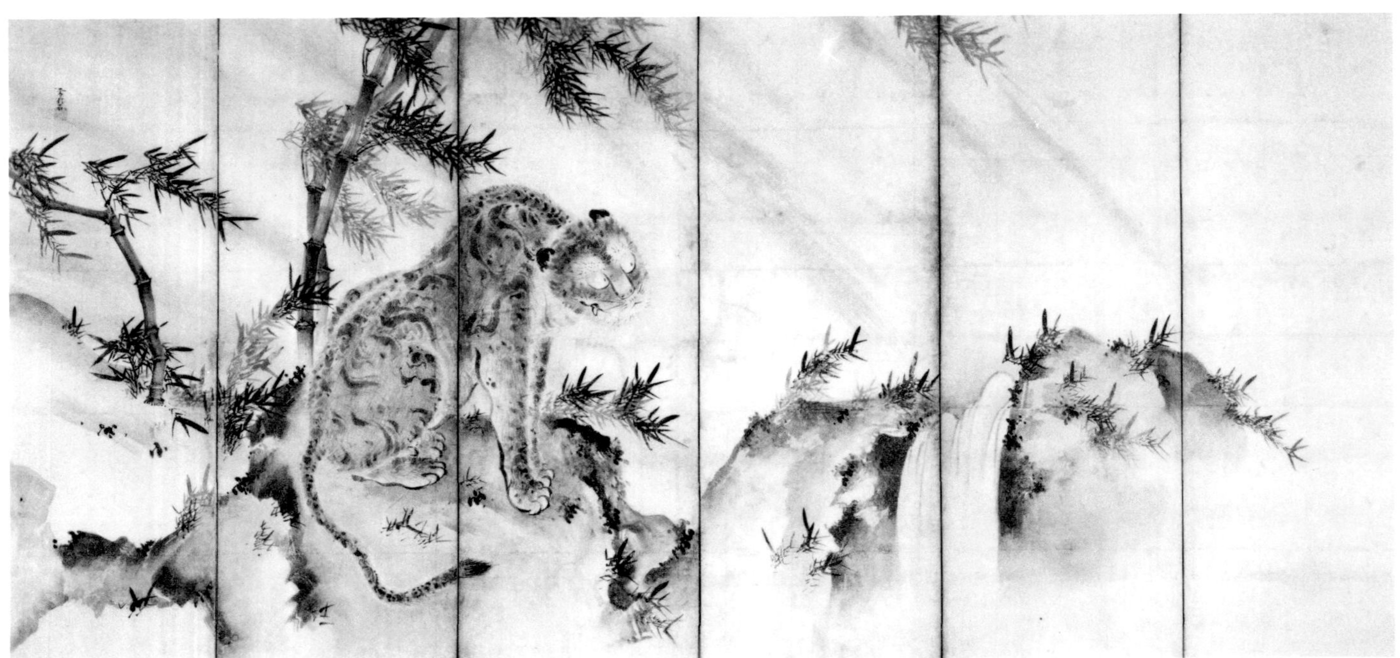

## 36
## Tiger and Dragon

*Sesson, 1504-1589?*
*Pair of six-fold screens; ink on paper*
*H. 157.2 cm. W. 339 cm., each*
*Ex collections: Mitsui H.; Satomi C.*
*Purchase from the J. H. Wade Fund 59.136-.137*

The few basic materials about Sesson's life have been well-known only since 1933[1]. Unlike Shūbun and Sesshū, he was an outlander living in the relatively remote Northern provinces of Hitachi and Iwashiro between present day Tokyo and Sendai. Perhaps his "provinciality" was a major source of strength, allowing him to develop his own manner without reference to the numerous and often uncreative artists at work in the home provinces around the capital, Kyoto. He was born about 1504 in Ōta (Hitachi) and was evidently there until at least 1546 when he was recorded as active in Aizu (Iwashiro). In 1542 he is believed to have written a short treatise on painting. In 1546 he instructed Ashina Mori'uji (1521-1580), a lord of the Aizu district, in the care and handling of scroll paintings, the lore of the Kundaikan catalogue of Chinese painting, and perhaps the techniques of painting. This may mark the time of his first real acceptance as an acknowledged master, a guess supported by his subsequent presentation of two sets of copies after Chinese paintings to a patron who may well have been the same Ashina. A few works, sealed Sesson, show a still conservative and stiff talent much indebted to Sesshū, among others. In 1550 he painted the typically realistic Zen portrait of the Priest Iten Sōsei. In 1563 he copied the "flung-ink" *(haboku)* landscape of the "Eight Views of Hsiao Hsiang" by the artist Ying Yü-chien, evidencing an exposure to one of the greatest if extreme and specialized examples of Chinese landscape painting. (See cat. no. 37 for a comparable work). This was followed by a copy in 1564 of the same subject by the even more important Chinese priest-painter, Fa Ch'ang (Mu-ch'i). By 1573 Sesson had gone to Tamura, Iwaki province (modern Fukushima prefecture) where he lived the solitary life of a Zen monk until his death. Six dated works from 1555 to 1589 bring his career to the age of 86 years. Probably it did not continue much longer.

There is much confusion and too much wishful thinking in filling out the chronology of Sesson's paintings with a remaining majority of undated but genuine examples. In general it can be said that he moved from a conservative, rather hard and prosaic style, to an extremely free, almost rollicking manner, joyfully exaggerated but supported by true virtuoso brushwork. These qualities are evident, whether in the tiny format of the famous small work, "The Wind Storm," or in the large scale of the multi-fold screen, a format he may well have first encountered under daimyo patronage after 1546.

Fortunately the date of the "Tiger and Dragon" screens can be fixed with some certainty. They are signed "Sesson painted," and sealed "Sesson" (Snow Village), "Shūkei", (*Shū*, with the same pronunciation as one of the components in the names of Shūbun and Sesshū; *kei*, continuing). The first seal is in the form of a vase, the second, a square with rounded corners and fine line seal characters. The same seals occur on only one dated painting, the "Iten Sōsei" of 1550. Since the late dated paintings use another set of seals, it seems reasonable to date the Cleveland pair about that date or perhaps within the ten succeeding years since the style of the screen is fully developed and distinctive Sesson. This manner was already described in principle in his treatise on painting. Before acknowledging his debt to Sesshū, but adding that he is himself alone, Sesson

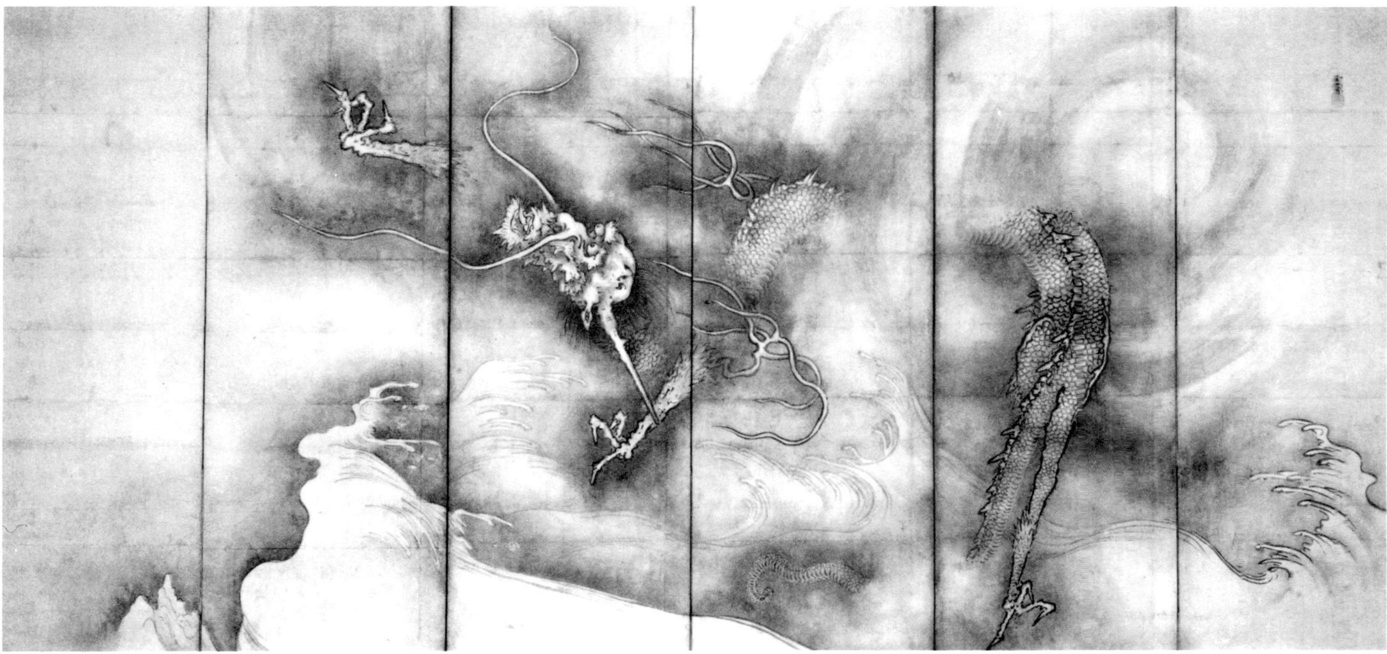

begins with a discussion of "ink method" and says: "Strong ink should come first, pale ink follows; among ten brush strokes, seven should be in strong ink, three in pale ink." This one can see in the "Tiger and Dragon." Dark tones predominate and are forced to the edges of shapes, making for a distinctly sharp and heightened impression of space and movement. Edges are crinkled or sinuous; there are few long sweeping forms except for the summary indications of wind and rainstorm. Rocks and water are particularly singled out for a more decorative treatment than had occurred before in Japanese monochrome painting in Chinese style.

The dragon, bamboo, and tiger, had long been favorite subjects of Chinese painting in the Sung dynasty. Such works found refuge in the Japanese Zen monasteries and there served as models for centuries. However, Sesson's "Tiger and Dragon" screens seem to be the earliest important Japanese rendition with little of the Chinese flavor left. They influenced numerous later painters; and Sesson's style seems to be carried on by the so-called Soga school. Sesson's treatise mentions the tiger and dragon category with the traditional explanation from the *Book of Changes*—the dragon arouses clouds (of water), the tiger evokes the wind. The aesthetic magic of the painted representation is called forth by the comparable capabilities of the tiger and dragon.

For militant lords and warriors, the tiger and bamboo—fierce, strong, and pliant—were admired symbols. The grim-humor of the ready tiger opposed to the wildly twisting dragon must have reminded the privileged spectator of now wild and then calculating sword play. The tiger is the most effective representation of that beast by the artist; and the bamboo is the peak of brush-artistry. The dragon has only one peer in Sesson's work, the small but remarkably active midget animal in the hanging scroll of the immortal Lü Tung-pin now in the Yamato Bunka Museum. Sesson's dragon is possessed by its powers, tense and full of movement before the watchfully waiting potential energy of the tiger.—SEL.

1. Fukui Rikichirō, "Sesson Shinron," (New Study on Sesson) *Suibokuga*, XX in the series, *Iwanami Kōza: Nippon Bungaku* (Tokyo, 1933). The chronology used here, as well as the excerpts from Sesson's treatise on painting, are derived from this basic study as translated by Wai-kam Ho.


Published:

*Nippon Teikoku Bijutsu Ryakushi* (Tokyo, 1908), pp. 160-61, pl. 146.

*Tokyo Teishitsu Hakubutsukan Bijutsu Reppin Shashin Mokuroku* (Tokyo, 1919), cat. nos. 2553-2554.

Imaizumi Yūsaku, *Shoga Kottō Sōsho* I (Tokyo, 1920), p. 138.

Fujikake Shizuya, "Tiger and Dragon by Sesson" *Kokka*, no. 737 (August, 1953), p. 224.

Sherman E. Lee, "The Tiger and Dragon Screens by Sesson," *The Bulletin of The Cleveland Museum of Art* 47, no. 4 (1960); pp. 65-69.

—————, *Japanese Decorative Style* (Cleveland, 1961), cat. no. 47.

—————, "Contrasts in Chinese and Japanese Art." *Journal of Aesthetics and Art Criticism*, XII (Fall, 1962), p. 5, figs. 5, 7.

Etoh Shun, "Sesson-ga no Isō," *Yamato Bunka*, no. 46 (January, 1967), pl. 14.

Shimada Shūjirō, ed., *Zaigai Hihō*, vol. 2, (Tokyo, 1969), pt. 1, pls. 134-135.

Nakamura Tanio, "Sesson to Kantō Suibokuga", *Nippon no Bijutsu*, VII, no. 63 (August, 1971), pl. 55.

Tanaka Ichimatsu and Nakamura Tanio, *Sesshū; Sesson*, Suiboku Bijutsu Taikei, VII (Tokyo, 1973), p. 189, fig. 19, pl. 123.

Shimizu Yoshiaki and Carolyn Wheelwright, eds., *Japanese Ink Painting* (Princeton, 1976), cat. no. 27.

*Japanese Screens from the Museum and Cleveland Collections* (Cleveland, 1977), cat. no. 7.

Nakamura Tanio and Wakisaka Atsushi, 'Sōjūga-Ryūko, Enkō,' *Nihon Byōbu-e Shūsei*, vol. 16 (Tokyo, 1977), p. 31, pls. 4, 16.

Shimada Shūjirō, *Suibokuga*, Zaigai Nihon no Shihō, vol. 3 (Tokyo, 1979), p. 150, colpls. 95-96.

Akazawa Eiji, *Muromachi no Suiboku*, Nihon Bijutsu Zenshū, vol 16 (Tokyo, 1980), pl. 59 (dragon), fig. 88 (tiger).

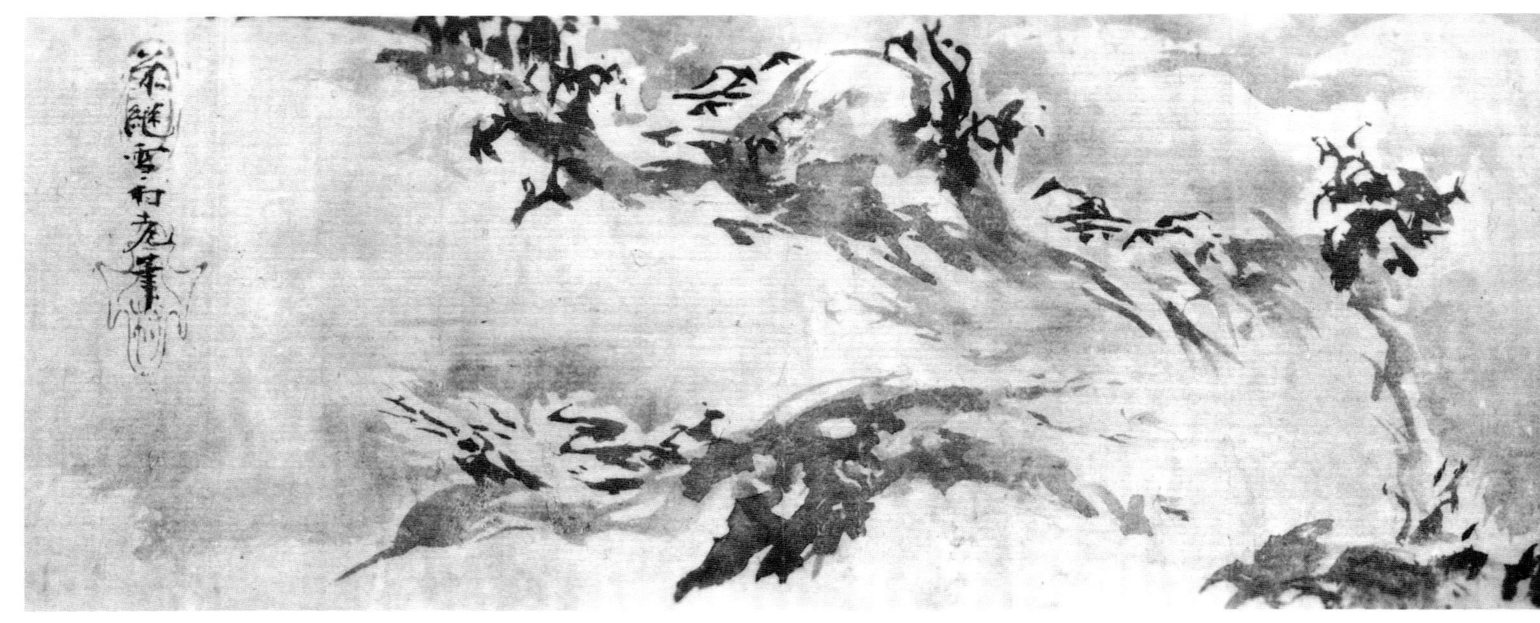

37

## Eight Scenes of the Hsiao and Hsiang Rivers

*Sesson, 1504-1589*
*Handscroll; ink on paper*
*H. 15.9 cm. L. 289.5 cm.*
*Ex collections: Bing, Paris; John D. Rockefeller 3rd*
*Gift of Sherman E. Lee in memory of John D. Rockefeller 3rd*
*79.77*

Sesson Shūkei painted the *Eight Views of Hsiao and Hsiang* frequently throughout his lifetime. Judging from his extant work it appears that it was a favorite subject—if not his most favorite. Of course like most Japanese painters Sesson had no idea of what this area south of Lake T'ung-ting actually looked like. He had never ventured to China to see the landscape where these two rivers met, preferring to satisfy himself with the terrain of eastern Japan instead. (see cat. no. 29).

The source of Sesson's interest in this theme and his visual depictions of it lay in the *Eight Views* paintings imported into Japan during the fourteenth and fifteenth centuries. Chinese paintings were avidly collected at that time of intense contact between the two countries—most significantly by the Ashikaga shoguns. Their collections contained many hundreds of Chinese paintings, the most renowned of which included *Eight Views* handscrolls by Mu-ch'i and Yü-chien, late thirteenth century monk-painters. While paintings by these men were unacceptable in China because of their loose, "unrefined" brushwork, they quickly came to be revered in Japan. Mu-ch'i's and Yü-chien's *Eight Views* became well-known, coveted objects among connoisseurs of the tea ceremony in Japan, a situation which led to their being cut into separate hanging scrolls, each depicting one of the traditional eight views. Their history, including the loss of several scrolls, is known mainly through the diaries of the men of tea and from copies made by generations of Japanese artists who were privileged to see them. By the end of the sixteenth century the names of Mu-ch'i and Yü-chien were synonymous not only with the very best Chinese "Zen" painting, but with the subject of the *Eight Views of Hsiao and Hsiang*.

Perhaps more important than the copies made of these handscrolls is the tremendous stylistic and compositional impact these paintings had on Muromachi artists, indeed upon the entire history of late Japanese painting. The specific nature of the imagery, brushstrokes, and artistic pedigree of those model paintings placed considerable technical demands upon the copyist. The artist was obliged to express something of the idiosyncratic spirit for which these two Chinese painters and their *Eight Views* scrolls were emblematic.

By the late fifteenth century a number of Japanese artists

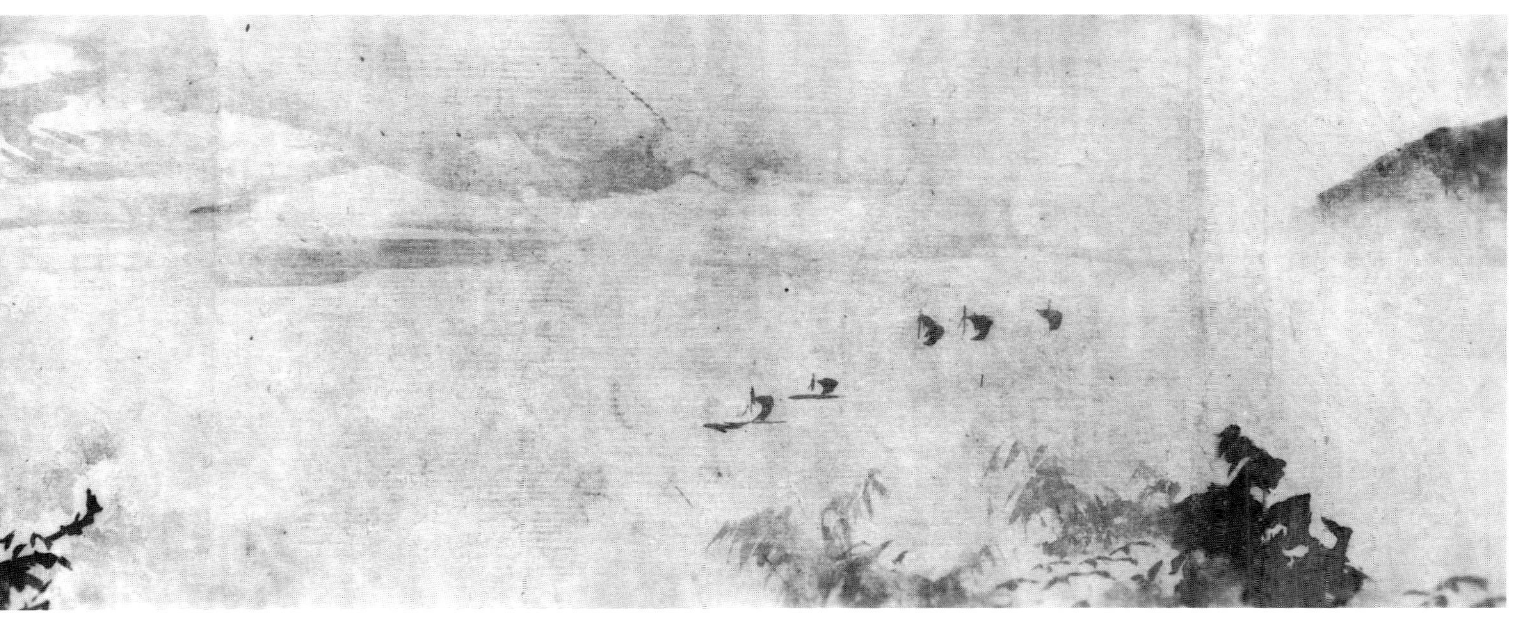

had executed *Eight Views* paintings in handscroll, hanging scroll, folding screen, and sliding door formats. Some of these were rigorously faithful to the originals while others altered the appearance of the originals sufficiently to merit recognition in their own right. They in turn became an integral part of the creative process which transformed Chinese ink painting imagery and style during the Muromachi era into authentic Japanese compositions.

Sesson's own efforts at mastering the *Eight Views* theme stem from his first-hand knowledge of specific model paintings, and from his study of early Japanese renditions of them. He knew paintings by Yü-chien, as well as Sesshū (1420-1506) and Sesshū-school compositions executed in response to the Yü-chien and Mu-ch'i models. His work indicates that his *Eight Views* paintings number at least fifteen, four of which are complete handscrolls. Among this group the Masaki and Cleveland museum examples are the most distinctive in compositional organization and brushwork. Both interpret what may be the identical Yü-chien *Eight Views* composition, or the later Cleveland handscroll may represent the artist's return to the subject with the Masaki scroll specifically in mind.

In any case this Cleveland piece illustrates the sequentially arranged views with an economy of description matched in only a few individual hanging scrolls depicting landscapes in the "broken ink" *(hatsuboku)* technique associated with Yü-chien. The adroit juxtaposition and layering of broad ink-wash areas define the people and the scenery of the Hsiao-Hsiang with a breadth of vision belying the 15.9 cm. height of the scroll. The varied shapes and "colors" of ink which Sesson's brush portrays, and their assured placement elucidate the subject just enough for the experienced viewer to recognize it. Once this is understood, one can return to marvel at the manner in which broad vistas and temporal transitions have been conveyed with beguiling economy and force. Sesson demonstrates his dynamic mastery of technique and history in a surprisingly large number of paintings. Among these, curiously, the breadth of vision seen in this very personal scroll, is best compared with another *Eight Views* painting, done at the age of eight-five on a six-panel folding screen in the Kuroda collection.—MRC


Published:

Sherman E. Lee, *Asian Art from the Collection of Mr. and Mrs. John D. Rockefeller 3rd,* (New York, 1975), cat. no. 35.

Tanaka Ichimatsu, *Sesshū-Sesson,* Suiboku Bijutsu Taikei, vol. 7 (Tokyo, 1973), pl. 108, pp. 146-47.

Nakamura Tanio, *Sesson to Kantō Suibokuga,* Nihon no Bijutsu, vol. 63 (Tokyo, 1970), figs. 40, 80.

Akazawa Eiji, *Muromachi no Suiboku,* Nihon Bijutsu, vol. 16 (Tokyo, 1980), figs. 75-77.

Hamada Takashi, et al., *Zaigai Bijutsu Kaiga,* Genshoku Nihon no Bijutsu, vol. 27 (Tokyo, 1980), figs. c22-25.

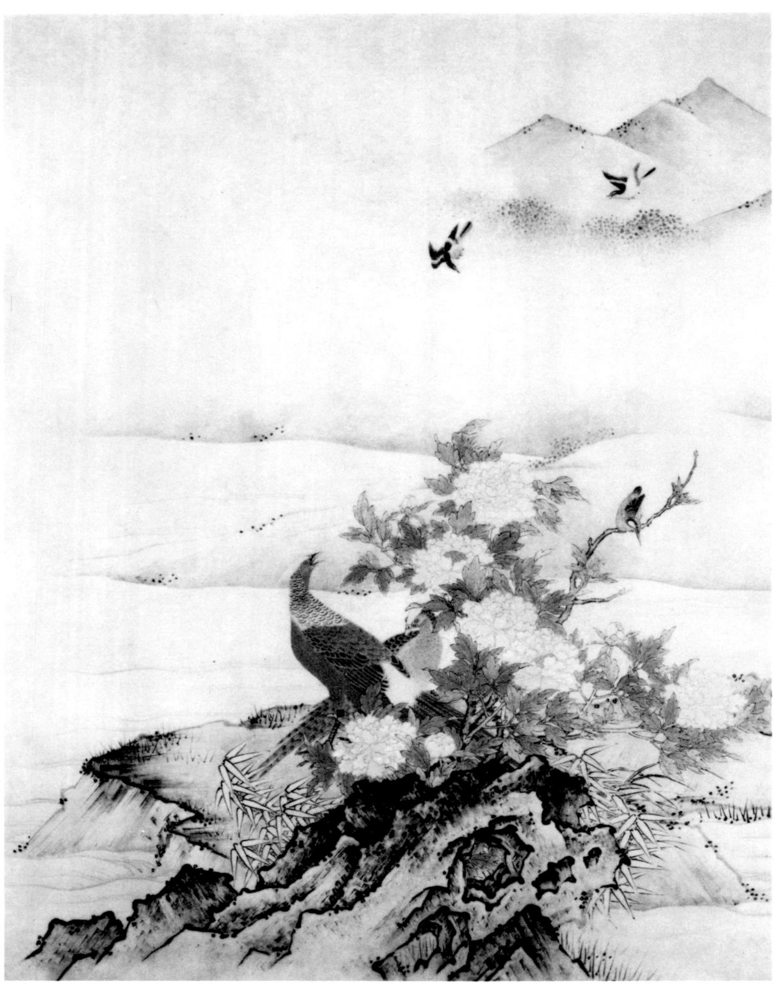

38

## Flowers and Birds in a Spring Landscape

*Kanō Motonobu (attributed to), 1476-1559*
*One of four panels mounted as hanging scrolls; ink and color on paper*
*H. 177.3 cm. W. 137.2 cm.*
*Purchase, Leonard C. Hanna Jr. Bequest 70.9*

Kanō Motonobu was the eldest son of Masanobu (1434?-1530?) and with his father is considered founder of the Kanō school, the Chinese influenced "academy" dominant in Japan until the eighteenth century. Motonobu was the father of Shōei (cat. no. 39) and like him official painter and arbiter of painting taste and history for the shogun and his court. Despite the importance and prominence of these early Kanō masters only one work a Hotei, is sure to be by Masanobu. No signed or documented works are known by Motonobu, and Shōei's certain works are limited to two sealed hanging scrolls with birds, flowers and rocks. Nevertheless, reasonably firm attributions to Motonobu are possible.

We know the artist received Zen training at the Reiun-in of Myōshin-ji in Kyoto and this connection has carried with it in modern opinion the group of paintings originally on the sliding doors of the Reiun-in, as well as others with more color at the Daisen-in of Daitoku-ji. These splendid and decorative paintings depict birds, flowers, trees, water and partial landscapes in a way wholly compatible with the style seen here. The Cleveland work is one of a set of four large hanging scrolls, originally sliding doors making a continuous composition. They share with the Daisen-in group bold and carefully structured brushwork in the manner of the Ma-Hsia school of Southern Sung China, sparing but effective use of color, and a carefully controlled placement of individual units of the composition to produce a markedly decorative effect. While this latter characteristic is indeed Japanese, it does derive in part from the Kanō family's study of such Ming dynasty decorative painters as Lu Chi, Yin Hung, Lin Liang and others—court painters of about 1500 whose works were exported to Japan. The Kanō genius lay in organizing these decorative compositions over such large areas as six-fold screens and sliding wall panels and making a particular virtue of contrasting near and far, empty space and complexity, in a way far more arbitrary and daring than the Chinese manner. Whether a part of this peculiarly Japanese decorative quality was derived from the courtly Tosa school derived from early *Yamato-e* is unknown; but the Kanō family did intermarry with the Tosa and succeeded them as heads of the Painting Bureau of the shogun's court. In any event, the early Kanō style as practiced by Motonobu and Shōei laid the foundations for the flowering of screen painting in the Momoyama period.—SEL

Published:

Harold P. Stern, *Birds, Beasts, Blossoms and Bugs: The Nature of Japan* (New York, 1976), cat. no. 12.

Tokyo National Museum, *Kanōha no Kaiga* (Tokyo, 1979), cat. no. 67.

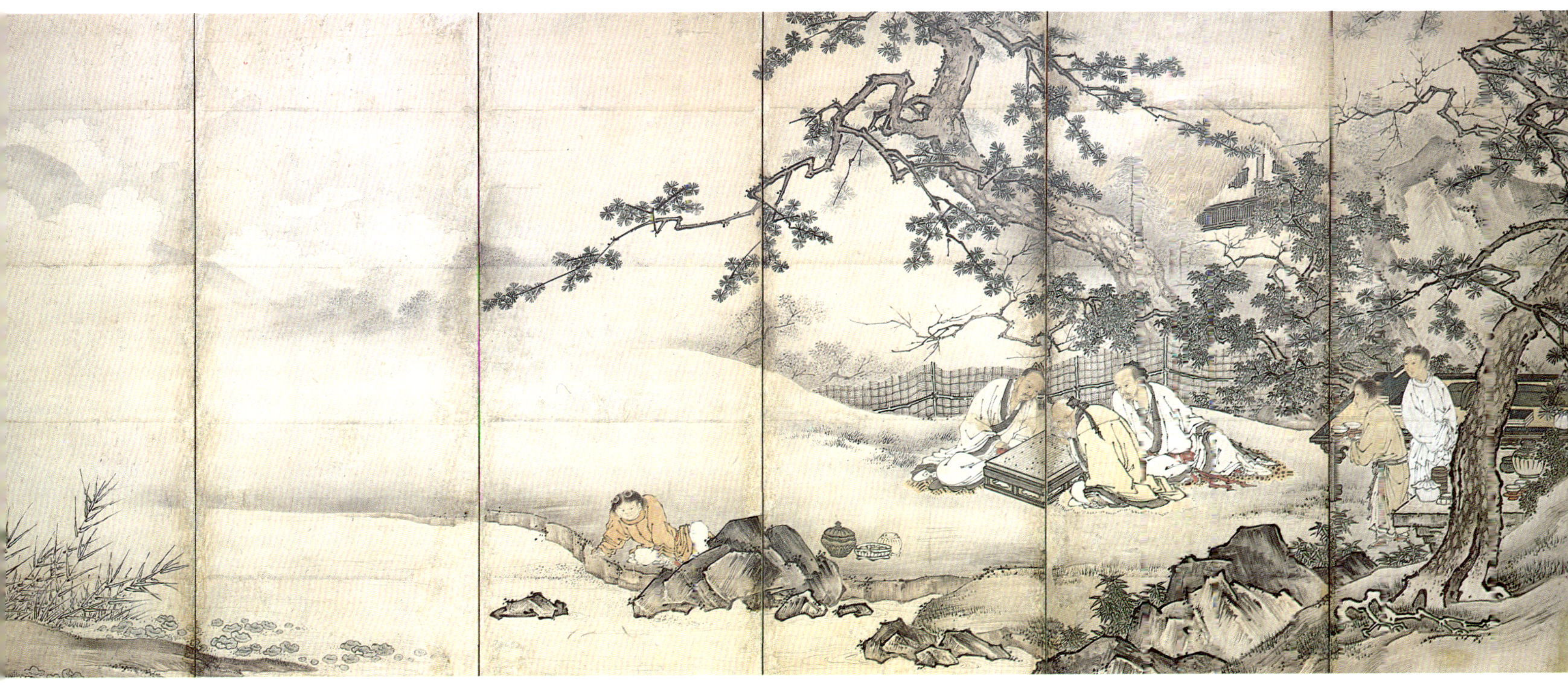

39

## The Four Accomplishments

*Kanō Shōei, 1519-1592*
*Pair of six-fold screens; ink and color on paper*
*H. 153 cm. W. 358.6 cm., each*
*Purchase, John L. Severance Fund 79.46*

The Four Accomplishments *(Kinki Shoga)* is a subject derived from the Chinese scholars' world and it became a standard manner of obeisance by Kanō painters to things Chinese. The four themes were: Painting, Calligraphy, Music, and the Game of War. The latter element was the game called *go* in Japan, a complicated translation of military maneuvers into a play of counters on a checkerboard. Those who wish to savor the complexities of this subtle and demanding game are urged to read the translation of Kawabata Yasunari's novel *The Master of Go.* It is no coincidence that Kawabata formed a first class collection of later Japanese paintings in the Chinese manner *(Nanga).* The Four Accomplishments in this pair of screens are both explicit—Painting and Go—and secretly alluded to—Calligraphy as an implicit adjunct to the depiction of Painting, and Music by the inclusion of a wrapped *ch'in* or *koto* half-hidden on the table beside the *go* players.

Thus the subject is only nominally the Four Accomplishments. The real subject is a group of figures in a landscape appropriate to scholarly life. This accounts for the noble pines, echoing the assumed character of the scholars and the rustic farm house setting alluding to the virtues of genteel poverty. The dominant subject is a seasonal one, for one screen can be seen as winter, the other as summer.

An important feature of the pair of screens is the accomplished brushwork. One can see the indebtedness of the artist to his father Motonobu and the decline in scale as well (see cat. no. 38). All is accomplished and superbly unified in a general view and soothing ambience. The mists across the top of the prunus tree, the staccato rhythms of the pines, the themes and variations to be observed in the modelling strokes of the rocks, and especially the unifying atmosphere of light and air, reveal a mastery of the newly developed Kanō idiom. What is lacking is what was present to a degree in Kanō Motonobu's work—large scale and daring composition. This was to come in the next generation of the Momoyama period under the patronage of Hideyoshi and his epigones, most particularly in the work of Kanō Shōei's son Eitoku.

The traditional attribution of these screens to Kanō Shōei is not firm, but reasonable in so far as we know the work of the period. The brushwork and rock forms are close to those in a pair of flower and rock paintings with the seal of the artist, the only near-documented works at hand. Their stylistic place between Motonobu and Eitoku is clear enough and no other recorded artist of the period from 1550-1590 except possibly Kanō Yukinobo (ca. 1513-1575) would have been capable of the easy command of early Kanō style to be seen in the "Four Accomplishments."—SEL

Published:
*Kokka,* no. 565 (December, 1937) pls. 3, 4.

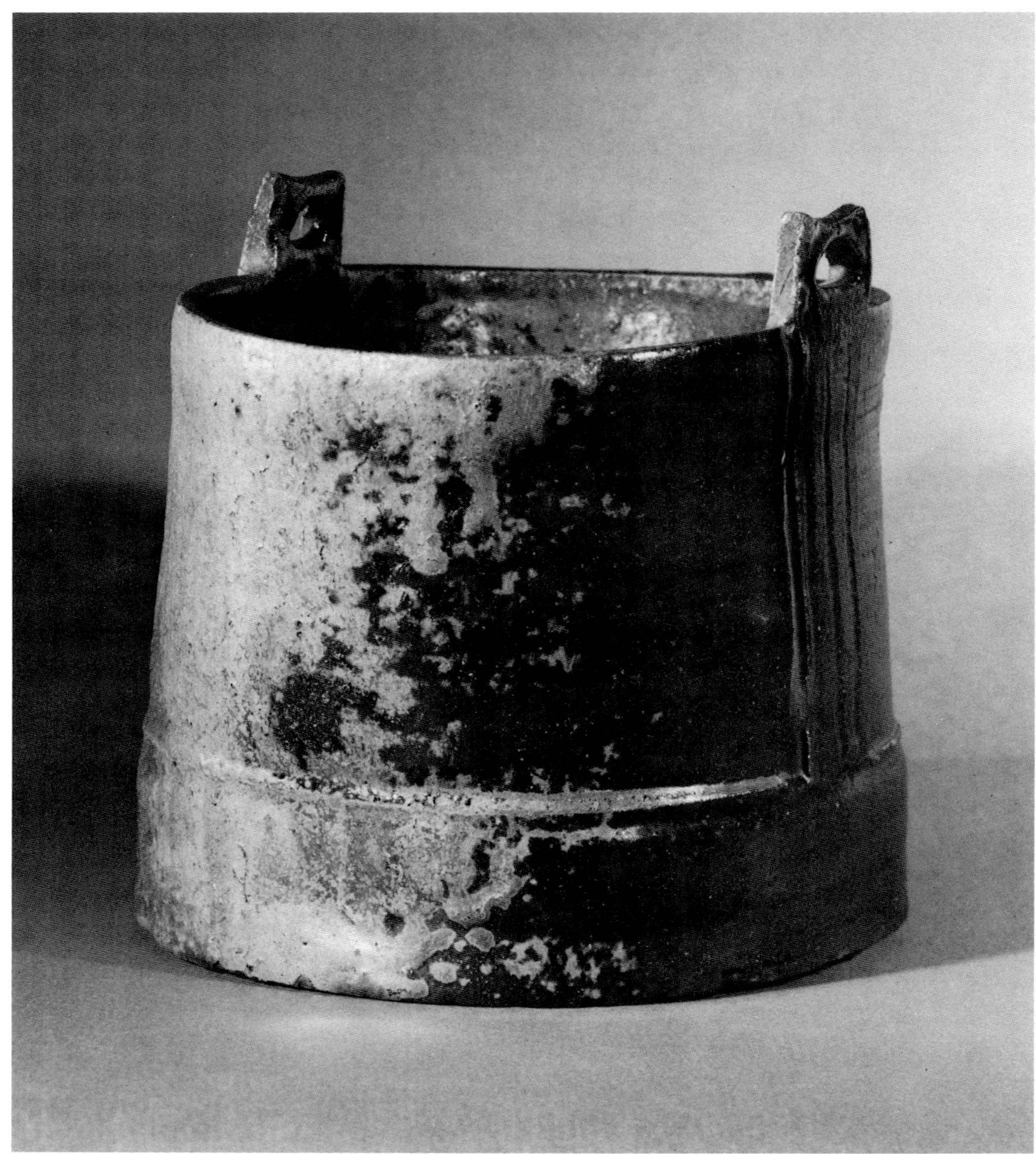

40

Water Jar (Mizusashi): Bizen ware

*Momoyama Period, early 17th century*
*Stoneware*
*H. 15.4. cm.*
*Purchase, John L. Severance Fund 73.17*

The wares of Bizen (modern Okayama prefecture) are direct descendants of the older folk wares of Heian times, typified by the old Sue wares. Most of the sixteenth and seventeenth century production was produced near the village of Imbe. Bizen and Imbe are more or less interchangeable designations of the products of the region. From the later Muromachi period on the kilns often catered to specific tea cermony requirements and the humble characteristics of old Bizen ware began to show a more sophisticated adaptation to the new requirements. The rusty brown color of its clay and iron glazes was well suited to the new aesthetics of tea. The most notable types produced were the fresh water jars *(mizusashi)* for replenishing the water in the kettle (see cat. no. 30) during the tea ceremony.

This example is in the form of a wooden water pail, *oni-oke* (devil-bucket), a common type found represented in numerous narrative scrolls with village scenes centered on the communal well (see cat. no. 19). This origin is in keeping with the "humble" aspirations of the tea ceremony. The olive to mustard glaze is developed from an application of a thick clay slip with high iron content. While the origin is from a wood prototype, the thrown clay character of the shape is strong and contrasts in a subtle way with the clay adaptations of the wood binding of the base and the upright pierced handles. The ceramic *mizusashi* sits more heavily on the ground than its light wooden counterpart. The subtle allusion to a different material common to folk culture and the tension between form and medium must have been a particularly satisfying conundrum to a tea master using this container. The dating of these Bizen wares is highly controversial and problematical since a Momoyama period date is preferable to an Edo period one. Good judgment and tea taste reticence suggest an early seventeenth century date for even the most excellent examples.—SEL

Published:

Katsura Matasaburō, *Jidaibetsu Ko-Bizen Meihin Zuroku* (Tokyo, 1973), colorpl. 85.

Sherman E. Lee, "Some Japanese Tea Taste Ceramics," *The Bulletin of The Cleveland Museum of Art* 60, no. 9 (1973): 274-75, fig. 6.

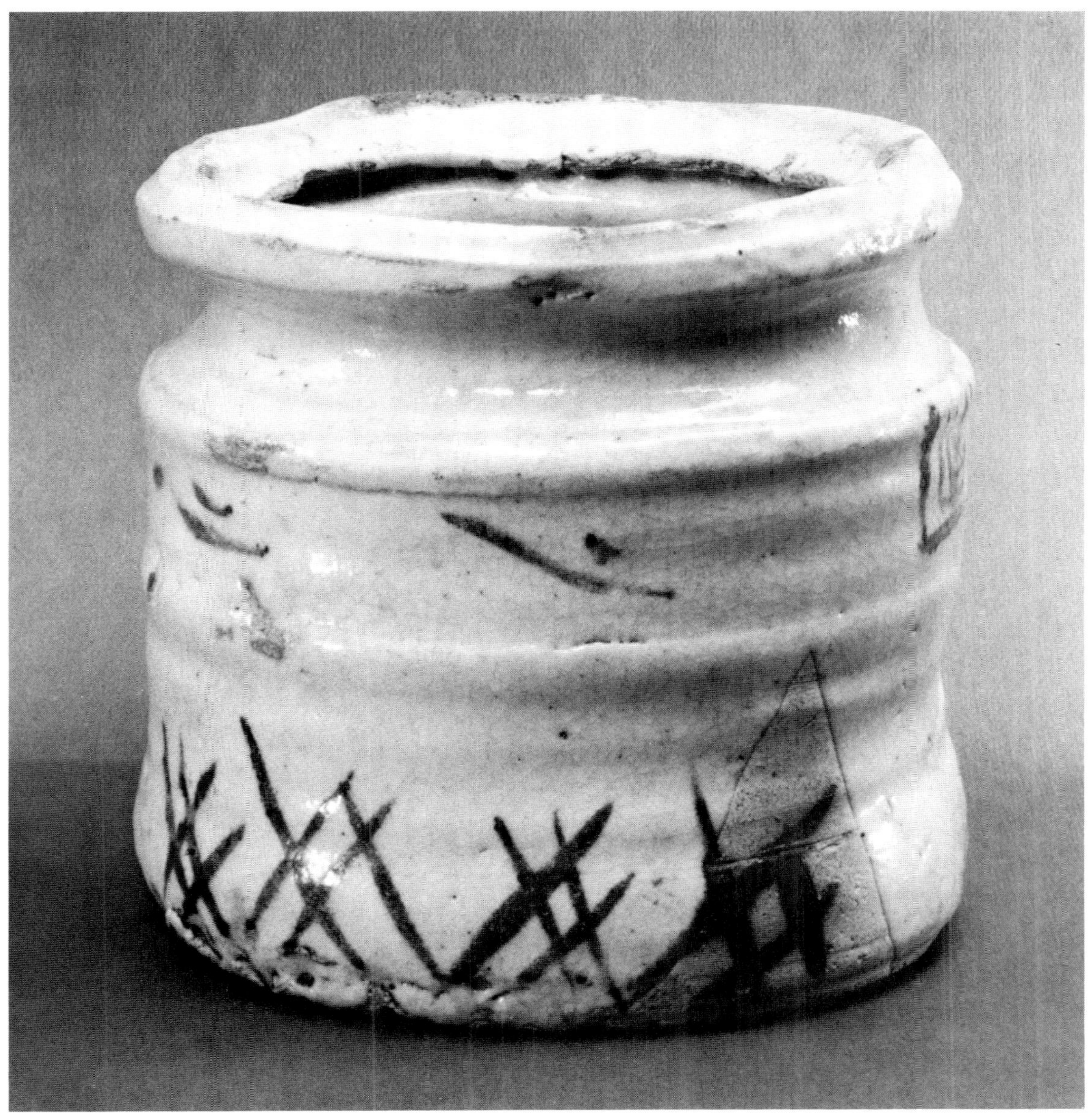

41
Water Jar (Mizusashi): Shino ware
*Momoyama Period, 16th century*
*Stoneware*
*H. 18.4 cm.*
*Purchase, John L. Severance Fund 72.9*

One of the most prized of tea ceremony objects is a Shino freshwater jar *(mizusashi)*. They are characteristically the most ceramic-like of tea wares and were made for or under the close supervision of knowledgeable tea devotees. The Shino wares were traditionally named for a famous tea master, Shino Sōshin who lived in the Daiei era (1521-27), and were made at the Mino province kilns just north of Seto. Thus the new wares were inheritors of the tradition of the Seto kilns active from the Kamakura period onwards. Some of the most famous of tea wares were made in the Mino area—Ki (yellow) Seto, Shino and Oribe (cat. no. 43). Standard Shino ware was marked by a thick milky glaze with sparsely brushed decoration in iron oxide, as in this *mizusashi*. Another variety, Nezumi (mouse) Shino, was characteristically gray in color with decoration in pale gray, almost white (see cat. no. 42).

The most famous of the Shino *mizusashi*, such as the Hatakeyama Museum example, called *Kogan* (ancient stream bank), display apparent weight, fluid plasticity in modelling, and rough, bold, and abbreviated decoration. The present example, one of the few early examples outside Japan, is free and plastic in its thrown shape, while the suggested weight and the brushed fence and panel decoration are lighter and more elegant than those of the pot called *Kogan*. The panel decoration is related to that often found on Oribe wares (see cat. no. 43). This may indicate a date slightly later than the Momoyama period.

The tea taste so well embodied in this water jar requires special study and close attention. Rough but not too rough; natural and free but with the clear evidence of human art (manufacture), these wares have now found a sympathetic audience—the modern artist-potter. The influence of such Japanese wares has been particularly marked in recent years.

—SEL

Published:
Fujioka Ryōichi, *Shino to Oribe*, Nihon no Bijutsu, vol. 51 (Tokyo, 1970), pl. 6.

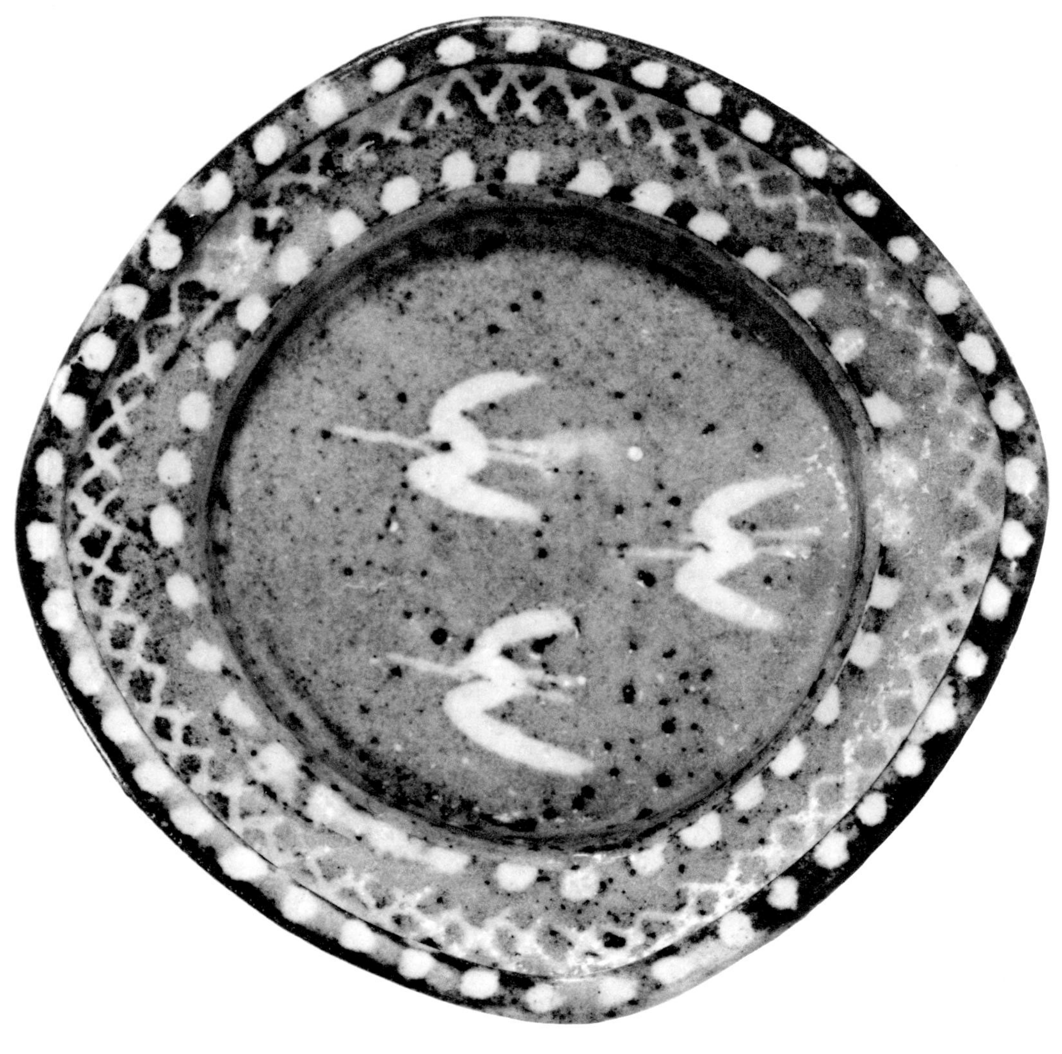

## 42
## Dish with Design of Three Wild Geese in Flight: Gray Shino ware

*Momoyama Period, ca. 1600*
*Stoneware*
*H. 5.4 cm.*
*Gift of Mrs. A. Dean Perry 59.35*

Gray Shino examples display somewhat richer decorative ambitions than the *E-shino* (painted shino) types. While numerous rectangular shaped dishes are known, the favored Gray Shino dish shape is neither rectangular nor circular but a varied and subtle compromise between the two extremes. Dishes of this size were usually made in sets of five as serving dishes for various occasions—from dining to tea ceremony occasions.
—SEL

Published:
Sherman E. Lee, *Japanese Decorative Style* (Cleveland, 1961), cat. no. 50.
Martin Lerner, "Tea-Ceremony Pottery and Export Porcelain," *The Bulletin of The Cleveland Museum of Art* 54, no. 9 (1967): 271, fig. 2.
Soame Jenyns, *Japanese Pottery* (London, 1971), pl. 53b.

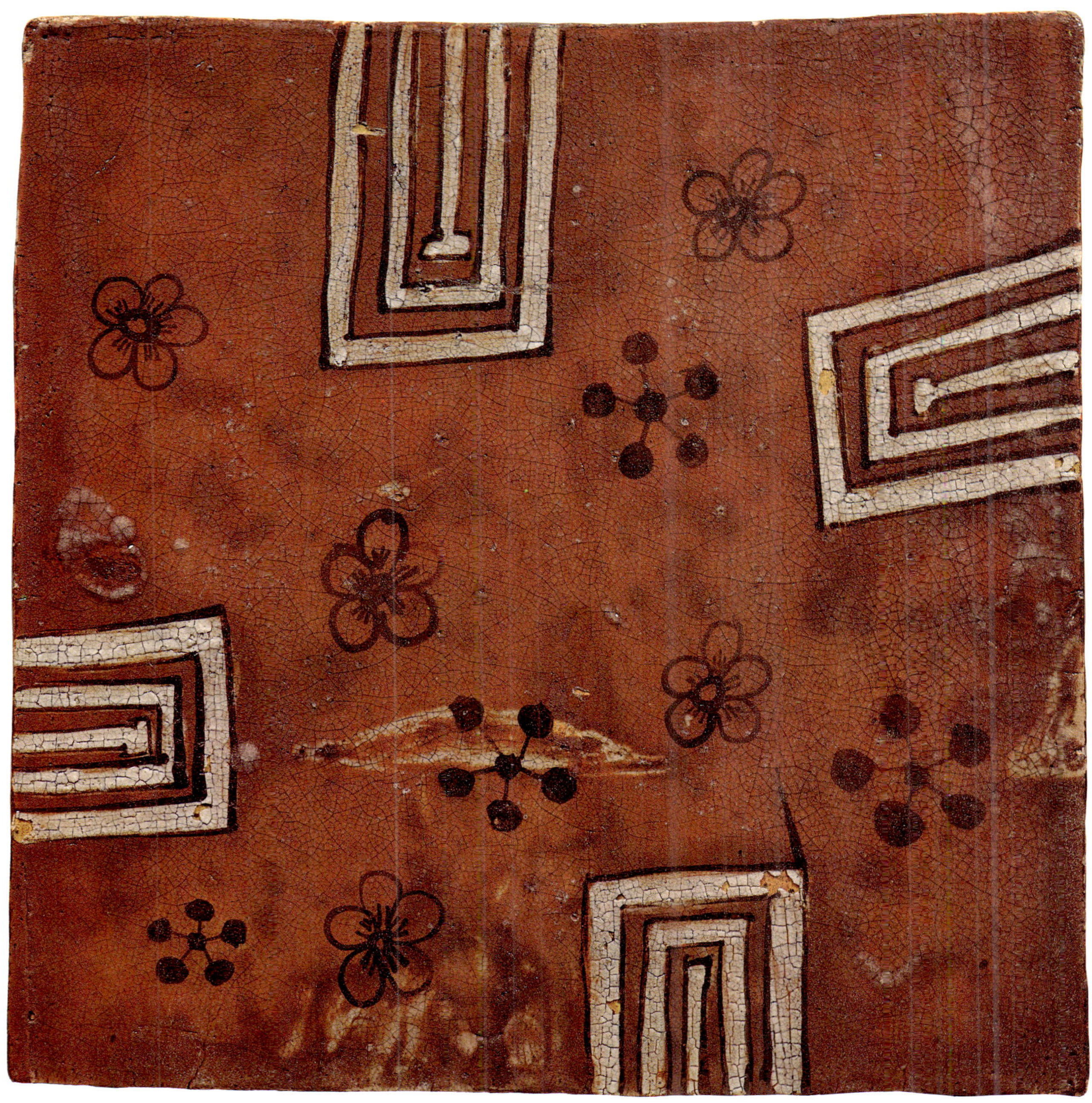

43

## Tile Platform for Tea in Summer: Red Oribe ware

*Momoyama Period, ca. 1600*
*Stoneware with painted slip decoration*
*H. 32.4 cm.*
*Ex collection: Higashi-Hongan-ji, Kyoto*
*Anonymous Gift 65.79*

Oribe ware is usually a combination of exposed cream-colored slip, green glaze, and iron oxide decoration in various shades of brown. Another less common variety is called Red Oribe and uses a rusty red glaze over cream and brown elements of the Oribe vocabulary. This particular example is not only rare because it is Red Oribe but because it is a tray or platform in the conformation of a tile. It is possible that the tile was used as a platform for the brazier used to heat the kettle for the tea ceremony.

The decoration uses standard elements of the Oribe style—rectangular, repeated panels, prunus blossoms, and water weed motifs. The calculated and mild asymmetry of the design is particularly happy on the square format; a more extreme play with balance would be appropriate on the cylindrical formats of bowls, ewers, and dishes.

The platform recalls the unglazed tiles characteristic of early earthenware architectural elements still extant from the Asuka and Nara periods, and this slight genuflection to the past may well have been in the mind of the designer of this particular ceramic.—SEL

Published:
Sherman E. Lee, *Tea Taste in Japanese Art* (New York, 1963), cat. no. 30.

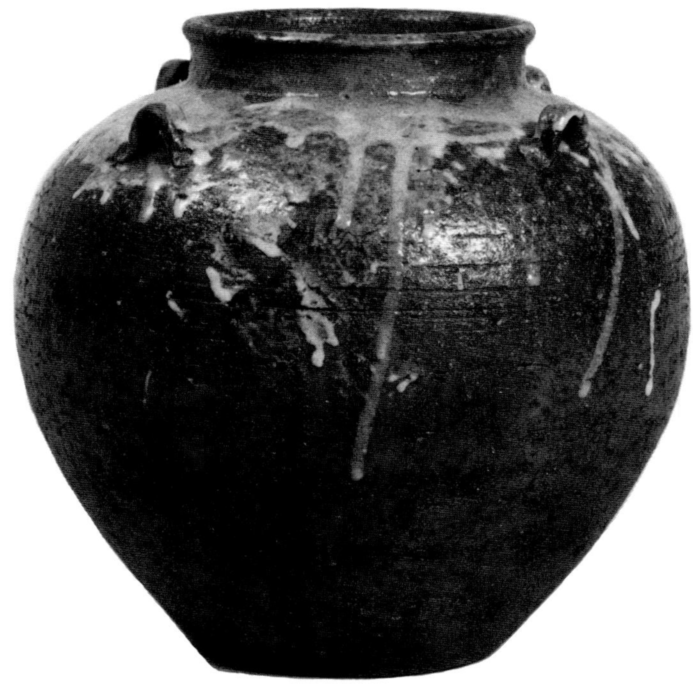

44

Tea Storage Jar: Shigaraki Type

*Nonomura Ninsei, ca. 1574-ca.1685*
*Glazed stoneware*
*H. 28.3 cm. Diam. 18.7 cm.*
*Ex collection: Maeda; Toyama*
*Purchase from the J. H. Wade Fund 78.6*

By the beginning of the sixteenth century the manufacture of storage jars *(tsubo)* and other vessels intended for sale to the burgeoning numbers of tea taste aficionados in the Kyoto-Nara-Osaka area was gaining tremendous momentum. Tea ceremony schools and styles proliferated, and in doing so attracted increasing numbers of followers. The destruction in the Ōnin wars (1467-77) of many valuable Chinese ceramics, previously established as the preferred tea ceremony utensils, further intensified the search for and "certification" of appropriate Japanese replacements. The exigencies of this selection process were to have a most salutary effect on Japanese art and connoisseurship.

By the mid-sixteenth century an increasingly sophisticated production, selection, and distribution system for Shigaraki wares was in operation (see cat. no. 31). Recognized tea masters sketched designs for individual pieces or sets of utensils which were subsequently executed on commission. Large orders placed by tea merchants also influenced the ceramic trade significantly. Pots were no longer actively "discovered," they were made to order and intentionally glazed to create desirable surface effects. The anonymous Shigaraki potter-farmer was replaced by an active professional potter.

These men and women labored individually or in modest "workshops" to fill the orders from Kyoto, Nara, and Osaka. An outgrowth of this system was the training of apprentices and, inevitably, a migration of talented potters to Kyoto at the beginning of the seventeenth century. They came from the Mino and Seto areas, Bizen, Shigaraki, and from Tamba, a "Six Old Kilns" site to the west of Kyoto.

Nonomura Ninsei was a native of Tamba, an agricultural valley whose storage jars not only resemble Shigaraki's coiled forms, but antedated Shigaraki's in their selection for use by early tea aesthetes. Ninsei's arrival in Kyoto early in the Edo period coincides with the establishment of kilns at the eastern edge of the city and the ensuing production of Kyoto ceramics (Kyoto *yaki*). Although best known and appreciated in Japan for his pieces decorated in bright polychrome enamels, Ninsei also produced more restrained pieces like this Cleveland storage jar.

The exact dates of Ninsei's life are not known. Judging from a few dated pieces and written documents however, he was active by mid-century at his Omuro kiln near Ninna-ji, thanks to the patronage of the influential tea master Kanamori Sōwa (1584-1656). Prior to this he had worked at Seto learning to make tea caddies, and at the Awataguchi kiln in Kyoto. He was active into the 1680's, his work including water containers, tea caddies, teabowls, and storage jars of superb technical sophistication. Among his stoneware storage jars with applied glazes are three "copies" *(utsushi)* of traditional tea storage jars, including this one now in Cleveland.

The wheel-thrown body of the Ninsei jar is taut, the wide neck topped by a thick everted lip. A thin white glaze skillfully splashed over the torso and loop-lugs, contrast dramatically with the orange-brown body. The surface has been scraped clean leaving a pocked surface, reminiscent of linear splits in earlier jars, and some horizontal lines created by large granules of sand and feldspar being dragged across the surface by a paddle as the pot was rotated. A large, characteristic "Ninsei" seal is impressed on the base as well as on Ninsei shards found at the Omura kiln site, attesting to his involvement at mid-century in producing *utsushi* wares. That the transformation of traditional Shigaraki ware is not sheer artifice, but a historically-conscious, technically orchestrated effort to create a viable Kyoto ceramic tradition can be learned from the fact that the clay body contains little—if any—Shigaraki clay. This Shigaraki style jar is reputed to have formerly belonged to the Maeda family of Kaga, important patrons of Ninsei. —MRC


Published:

Kawahara Masahiko, *Ninsei*, Nihon Tōji Zenshū, vol. 27 (Tokyo, 1976), pl. 15.

Mitsuoka Tadamari, ed., *Edo*, Sekai Tōji Zenshū, vol. 6 (Tokyo, 1976), pl. 120.

Louise Allison Cort, *Shigaraki, Potters' Valley* (New York, 1979), fig. 176.

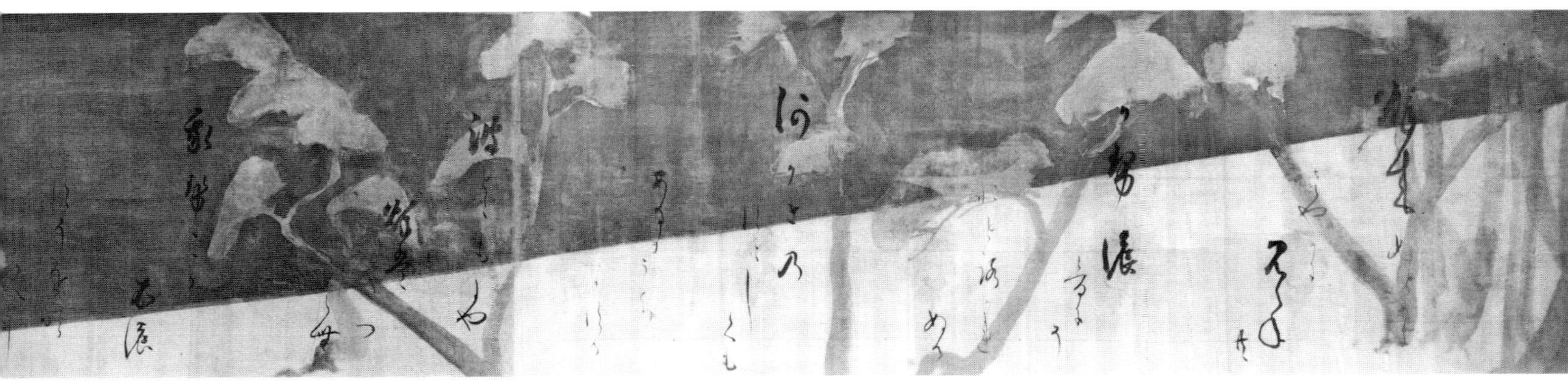

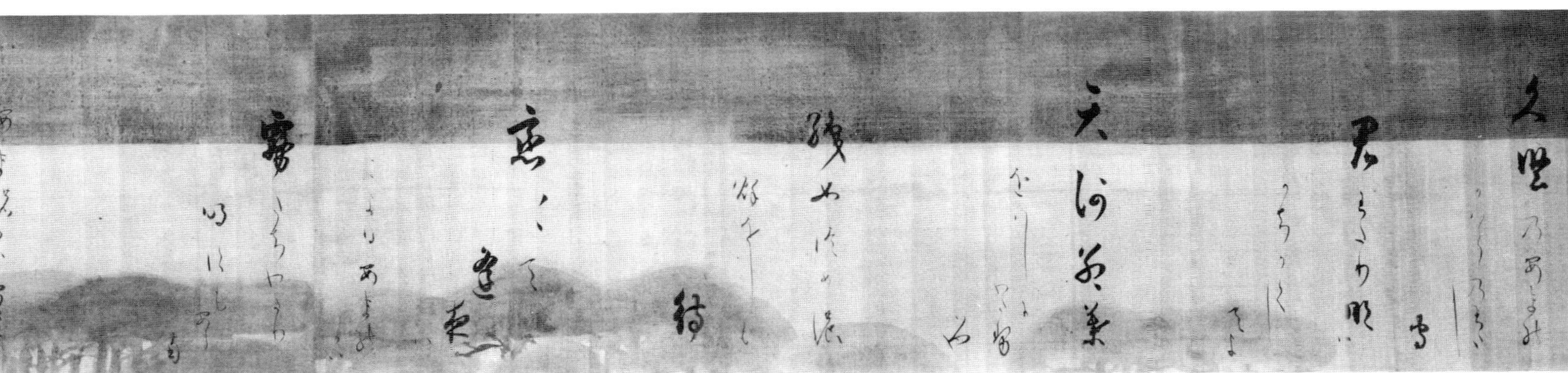

45

## Poem Scroll of Kokinwakashū

*Painting attributed to Nonomura Sōtatsu, 1576-1643?*
*Calligraphy by Hon'ami Kōetsu, 1558-1637*
*Handscroll; ink and color on silk over gold ground paper*
*H. 32.7 cm. L. 543.4 cm.*
*Ex collection: Hara Tomitarō, Yokohama*
*Purchase, Leonard C. Hanna Jr. Bequest 72.67*

Some of the most striking and attractive products of the Sōtatsu-Kōetsu school of the early seventeenth century are the decorated poem handscrolls executed in gold, silver and ink on paper, or more rarely on silk, In this scroll the calligraphy of a section from the *Kokinwakashū* is freely written in Kōetsu's characteristic cursive style while the pine tree background decor is executed in markedly bold, wet and free washes of gold and silver by Sōtatsu. The daring of the composition with its initial view of the pines from below, a final view of pine tops from above, and the dominant use of arbitrary diagonals representing land and clouds, recalls the famous "Ivy Lane" pair of screens by Sōtatsu. Also characteristic of that master is the adding of ink to wet pooled washes, the technique known as *tarashikomi.*

This bold and expressive decorative style, combining pictorial motifs with calligraphy that included literary references to the aristocratic tastes of the Heian period, was the invention of Kōetsu and Sōtatsu and was practiced by the colony of artists and craftsmen gathered by Kōetsu at Takagamine, in northwest Kyoto. The subtle reverberations of the past, presented in a new and daring mode, ushered in a second renaissance of Japanese decorative style (later called the Rimpa school) continued by Kōrin and Hōitsu among many others.

—SEL

Published:
Yashiro Yukio, "Zuihitsu Sōtatsu, II," *Yamato Bunka* 11 (1953), fig. 2, p. 45.
Kokka sha, ed., *Kōetsu sho Sōtatsu Kingin Doro-e,* 2 vols. (Tokyo, 1978), vol. 2, pl. 6.
Tokyo National Museum, *Nihon no Sho* (Tokyo, 1978), cat. no. 261.

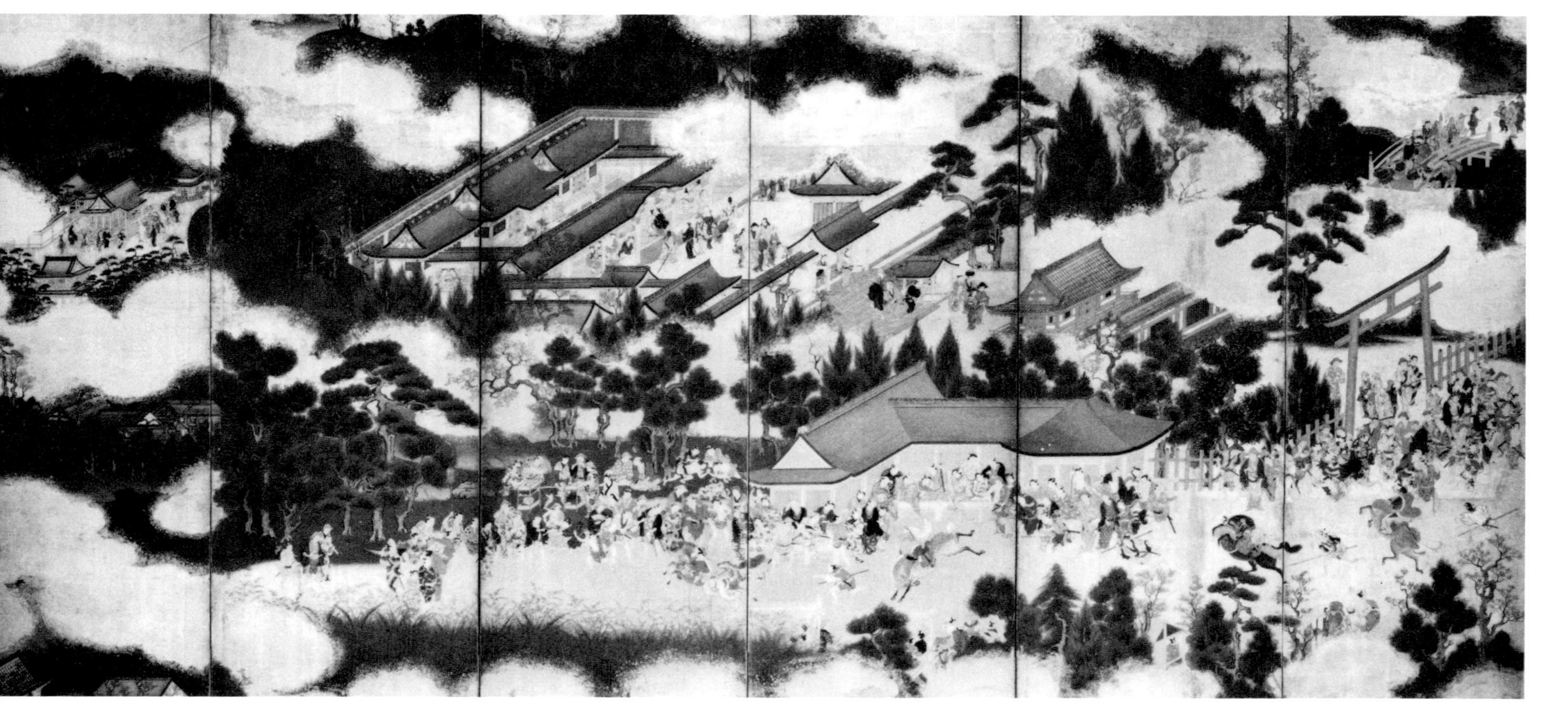

## 46
## Horse Race at the Kamo Shrine

*Edo Period, 17th century*
*Pair of six-fold screens; ink and color on gold-ground paper*
*H. 161 cm. W. 362 cm., each*
*Ex collections: Fuse Ryōen, Hyogo; Ohara Tadatake, Osaka; Wada Gozaemon, Hyogo.*
*Purchase from the J.H. Wade Fund 76.95-.96*

The most famous horse race of ancient Japan is the one held annually on the fifth day of the fifth month at Kami (upper) Kamo Shrine just north of the Imperial Palace in Kyoto. Kami Kamo Shrine, with its partner, Shimo (lower) Kamo Shrine, was one of the oldest and most venerated of Shinto shrines in Japan. The two shrines are closely woven into Japanese history and the elaborate rituals and festivals of Shinto were an important part of Japanese society and its calendar. The continuity of the imperial court, which was the visible center of ritual, was thought to depend upon the maintenance of the traditions of Shinto. From very early times the running of horses seems to have been a part of festivals at both shrines.

The relatively few known direct representations of the Kamo races come from the time of the Momoyama (1573-1615) and early Edo periods (1615-1716). There were at least three schools of painting ready and able to deal with this lively subject. The Tosa School was principally associated with traditional and conservative courtly patronage, and drew its inspiration from the old narrative handscroll tradition characterized by an interest in native landscape and architecture, numerous figures in varying degrees of action, or if courtly types, studied inaction. Costume was particularly important to such painters, for the details of costume not only denoted rank but also a traditional Japanese fascination with the patterns and colors of textiles.

The second group of painters was that of the Kanō School, initially devoted to Chinese methods of depicting Chinese scenes of landscape, "fur and feather," history, or legend. By the Momoyama period the purity of their Chinese manner had been modified by the demands of their warrior-ruler patrons for Japanese narrative scenes and landscapes. To them fell the principal task of decorating the new castles set up under the patronage of the Momoyama dictator Hideyoshi and his successors, the Tokugawa shoguns with their capital at Edo (Tokyo) but with their vassals scattered throughout Japan in such important castles as those at Osaka, Nagoya, and Kyoto. The huge quantities of sliding doors and folding screens needed on short notice for these vast constructions led to the employment of assistant painters, the town painters *(machi-eshi)*.

The town painters produced works for one and all—lesser warriors, merchants, innkeepers, and the like. Borrowing from both Tosa and Kanō styles, they developed a free and easy, somewhat folkish and abbreviated manner suitable to scenes of everyday life, local architecture, and landscape, as well as

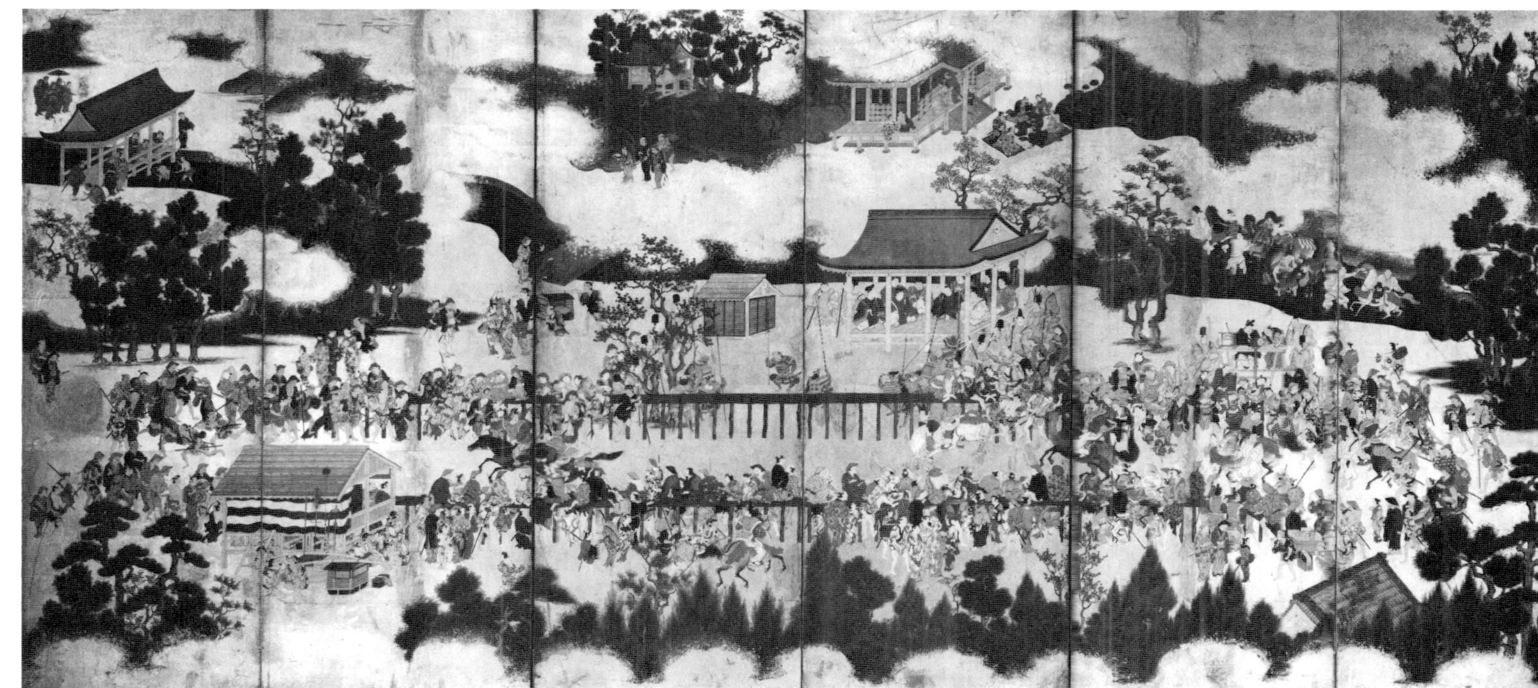

the more hallowed traditional subjects. If one places these three schools of painters at the service of a new and burgeoning curiosity about life as it existed, the results are splendid, decorative, and observant genre paintings such as this pair of screens.

The two Kamo festival screens form a continous composition from the right to left. The race begins in the far right panels and carries into the next screen past the gate of Kami Kamo Shrine, ending at the outbuildings below the shrine itself. After the initial throng, a more open area follows, dominated by a bark-roofed and pillared pavilion occupied by formally attired male members of the court and the Imperial entourage. This group is isolated by a screen of guards, either in carefully starched court costumes or in full military armor. From this point onto the left, the middle and lower classes dominate the proceedings and decorum progressively weakens. Some spectators are to be found in increasing numbers on the inner side of the railings, and some even interfere with the horses. As the race progresses into the left-hand screen the horses are prodded by stave-bearing samurai. The resulting rearing and bucking loosens the riders' grips and one is flung off his mount—to the evident hilarity of the motley crowd. Towards the end, beneath the august precincts of the main shrine, spectator participation becomes free and dominant; the race itself is ended. Still the idea of point and counterpoint continues, moving from those directly involved in the end of the race to those more interested in vendors of drink and food, or to a singularly disinterested group wholly concerned with a contest of arm wrestling.

Above the hurly-burly of the race stands the Kamo Shrine complex, its rigorous geometry at odds with the wild activity below. Here more decorous groups of figures quietly parade, some paying obeisance to the deity of Kamo, while others seem to be merely showing their holiday costumes. This major architectural, geometric element is echoed in other parts of both screens; it is almost equal in emphasis with the landscape and the people. A unified effect is created by the copious use of gold leaf squares for the ground and clouds with heightened accents of sprinkled gold at the soft edges of the cloud patterns. The overall effect of gorgeous decoration inherited from the Momoyama tradition is impressive, but this is supported by an intense interest in detailed narrative and characterization. The subject, style, and details of costume all substantiate the traditional dating of these screens to the Kanei era (1624-1644).—SEL


Published:

"Horse Race at Kamo," *Kokka*, no. 589 (December 1939), pls. 3, 4, 5.

Kyoto National Museum, *Kyō-meisho Fūzoku-zu* (Kyoto, 1970), cat. no. 9.

Sherman E. Lee, "Horse Racing at Kamo Shrine," *The Bulletin of The Cleveland Museum of Art* 64, no. 8 (1977): pp. 255-274.

Takeda Tsuneo, ed., *Shōheiga*, Zaigai Nihon no Shihō, vol. 4 (Tokyo, 1980), nos. 106, 107.

# Chronology

*Asuka Period: 552-645*
*Early Nara Period (Hakuhō): 645-710*
*Late Nara Period (Tempyō): 710-794*
*Early Heian Period (Kōnin): 794-897*
*Late Heian Period (Fujiwara): 897-1185*
*Kamakura Period: 1185-1333*
*Nambokuchō Period: 1333-1392*
*Muromachi Period: 1392-1573*
*Momoyama Period: 1573-1615*
*Edo Period: 1615-1868*

# Trustees of The Cleveland Museum of Art

James H. Dempsey, Jr., President
George P. Bickford
George M. Humphrey II
James D. Ireland
Mrs. Edward A. Kilroy, Jr.
Severance A. Millikin
Mrs. R. Henry Norweb
George Oliva, Jr.
A. Dean Perry
Mrs. Alfred M. Rankin
Daniel Jeremy Silver
Mrs. Seth C. Taft
Paul J. Vignos, Jr.
Alton W. Whitehouse, Jr.
John S. Wilbur
Lewis C. Williams
Norman W. Zaworski

# Founders and Friends of Japan House Gallery

Lily Auchincloss*, Chairman
Mrs. Vincent Astor*
Mr. and Mrs. J. Paul Austin*
Mr. and Mrs. Armand P. Bartos*
Mr. and Mrs. Jack N. Berkman*
Mr. Joe Brotherton*
Dr. and Mrs. Walter A. Compton*
Mrs. Cornelius Crane*
Mr. and Mrs. Edgar M. Cullman, Jr.
Mr. and Mrs. Lewis B. Cullman
Mr. and Mrs. Richard M. Danziger*
Mr. and Mrs. C. Douglas Dillon*
Mr. and Mrs. Peter F. Drucker*
Mrs. Frederick L. Ehrman
Mrs. Richard Ellis
Mr. John L. Ernst
Mr. and Mrs. Myron S. Falk, Jr.*
Mr. and Mrs. Charles A. Greenfield*
Mr. Louis W. Hill, Jr.*
Mr. and Mrs. William H. Johnstone*
Mr. Yale Kneeland III*
Mr. and Mrs. E. J. Landrigan
Mrs. H. Irgens Larsen*
Lucia Woods Lindley*
Ms. Jean C. Lindsey*
Mr. and Mrs. Henry A. Loeb*
Mr. and Mrs. Richard D. Lombard
Mr. Stanley J. Love*
Mr. C. Richard MacGrath
Edward John Noble Foundation
Mr. and Mrs. S. Morris Nomura*
Margot Paul*
Mr. and Mrs. Joe D. Price*
Mr. and Mrs. James D. Robinson, III*
Mrs. John D. Rockefeller 3rd*
Mr. and Mrs. Sen Sōshitsu*
Mr. and Mrs. Isaac Shapiro
Mrs. Aye Simon*
Mr. and Mrs. Stephen Simon*
Mr. Irwin M. Stelzer
The Florence Loucheim Stol Foundation
Mr. and Mrs. Donald B. Straus*
Miss Alice Tully
Mrs. Arnold L. van Ameringen*
Mr. Henry P. van Ameringen
Mrs. Lila Acheson Wallace*
Mr. Richard W. Weatherhead*

*Founder

# Officers of Japan Society

Honorary Chairman
David Rockefeller

Chairman
The Hon. Robert S. Ingersoll

President
David MacEachron

Vice Chairmen
Lily vA. Auchincloss
Michael J. O'Neill
The Hon. William W. Scranton

Vice President
John K. Wheeler

Treasurer
Mark E. Buchman

Secretary
Robert B. Radin

# Advisory Committee on Arts

Porter A. McCray, Chairman
Lily Auchincloss
Richard S. Cleveland
Arthur Drexler
Dr. Jan Fontein
Dr. Cal French
Martin Friedman
Dr. Sherman E. Lee
William S. Lieberman
Dr. Howard A. Link
Dr. Miyeko Murase
Dr. John M. Rosenfield
Miss Jean Schmitt
Henry Trubner

# Committee on Care and Handling

Abe Mitsuhiro
Iguchi Yasuhiro
Oba Takemitsu
Sugiura Takashi